GLUTEN-FREE BREAD BAKING FOR BEGINNERS

SEEDED MULTI-GRAIN ROLLS, PAGE 44

gluten-free bread baking
FOR BEGINNERS

The Essential Guide to Baking Artisan Loaves, Sandwich Breads, and Enriched Breads

Silvana Nardone

Photography by Elysa Weitala

ROCKRIDGE PRESS

I dedicate this cookbook to all of you who
have been waiting to sink your teeth into bread
once again and to my son, Isaiah, whose gluten
intolerance made me a better baker.

For general information on our other products
and services or to obtain technical support,
please contact our Customer Care Department
within the United States at (866) 744-2665, or
outside the United States at (510) 253-0500.

Rockridge Press publishes its books in a variety of
electronic and print formats. Some content that
appears in print may not be available in electronic
books, and vice versa.

TRADEMARKS: Rockridge Press and the
Rockridge Press logo are trademarks or reg-
istered trademarks of Callisto Media Inc. and/
or its affiliates, in the United States and other
countries, and may not be used without written
permission. All other trademarks are the prop-
erty of their respective owners. Rockridge Press
is not associated with any product or vendor
mentioned in this book.

Interior and Cover Designer: Jami Spittler
Art Producer: Sue Bischofberger/Meg Baggott
Editor: Reina Glenn
Production Editor: Matthew Burnett
Production Manager: Jose Olivera

Photography © 2021 Elysa Weitala; food styling
by Malina Syvo
Author photograph courtesy of Stephen
Scott Gross
Cover: Classic Sourdough Loaf, page 104

ISBN: Print 978-1-648-76312-0
        eBook 978-1-648-76313-7
R0

CONTENTS

INTRODUCTION

When my son Isaiah was diagnosed with gluten intolerance, I owned an Italian bakery full of 50-pound bags of glutenous flour. As his mother, I felt guilt and confusion. Did I cause Isaiah's gluten intolerance by feeding him endless amounts of gluten? While the answer, medically speaking, is no, I couldn't help but feel responsible for a diagnosis that would change his life—and mine—forever. When I asked Isaiah what food he was going to miss the most, he said corn bread. I thought I was lucky that he'd chosen a recipe that already contained one naturally gluten-free ingredient: cornmeal. I was wrong. When I tried to recreate it without gluten, recipe after recipe turned out crumbly and tasteless. I knew in that moment that I had to rethink the way I was baking.

That set me on a journey to make a gluten-free flour that could substitute cup for cup for traditional all-purpose flour. It took me months of testing different flour and starch ratios, but eventually I made a corn bread so tasty that he devoured almost an entire loaf. The success inspired me to recreate all of his favorite foods, including chocolate chip cookies, pizza, and handmade pasta. I even made him a gluten-free birthday cake.

But despite my success, the one thing I kept failing at was sandwich bread. Each day, my recipe testing resulted in sunken, gummy loaves that were heavy as bricks. Isaiah would come home from school and pick up the loaf I had baked only to set it back down, disillusioned once again. It was years later that, in a moment of desperation, I threw the kitchen sink at it—every ingredient I had learned could help achieve a beautiful loaf of gluten-free bread combined with every technique I had been working on to give bread structure and texture. Thirteen ingredients later, I could finally send Isaiah off to school with a sandwich for lunch, just like every other fifth grader.

But I had more work to do. Sure, I celebrated that loaf with more bread recipes, like rolls and baguettes, but I knew I had to cut down the intimidatingly long ingredient list. Off and on for the next few years, I challenged myself to make gluten-free bread baking easier—and less stressful—for myself and anyone else who wanted to make bread at home. I also wanted to make sure the techniques I used were achievable for anyone stepping into bread baking—let alone gluten-free bread baking—for the first time.

In *Gluten-Free Bread Baking for Beginners*, I demystify how to make a loaf of bread. My experimentation taught me that certain well-known techniques are no longer necessary, like activating yeast before adding it to a recipe. Just eliminating that one step saves time and allows you to prep your bread flours in advance. Unlike traditional bread that requires gluten development through kneading, there's no gluten to develop in gluten-free bread baking, so I cut out all those complicated steps, creating the ultimate no-knead method. This is the modern way of bread baking, gluten-free for all.

PART 1

GLUTEN-FREE BREAD 101

I'm so happy you've decided to join me on my gluten-free bread baking adventure. In this section, I will share everything you need to know, from understanding how gluten-free bread works to what I use in my flour blends in place of gluten. I've also written a step-by-step guide to the gluten-free bread baking process and, of course, a troubleshooting section if you run into any bread making challenges along the way.

CHAPTER 1

ALL ABOUT GLUTEN-FREE BREAD BAKING

Since I first started baking gluten-free 14 years ago, much has changed in the gluten-free marketplace. Now, it's not uncommon to find dozens of gluten-free flours, starches, and binders available at your local supermarket. As you practice your bread baking, you'll learn what works best for you. It's a skill that takes experimentation and gets better over time as you learn about your kitchen environment, your baking equipment, and your own aptitudes. But first, you have to learn the basics. Let's get started.

How Does Gluten-Free Bread Work?

Understanding the science of gluten in traditional bread baking teaches you what elements you need to keep and what you can leave behind when you go gluten-free. Before you step into your kitchen, make sure you have a firm grasp on what gluten does so you can replicate it in your gluten-free bread.

Understanding Gluten

Gluten is a combination protein—made of gliadin and glutenin—found in some grains, including wheat, barley, and rye. Gliadin and glutenin proteins bind to each other, giving bread dough its stretchy quality and the finished loaf its quintessential chew. When you add water to flour to make bread dough, the proteins activate. Mixing and kneading the dough creates long, strong, sticky strands of gluten that give bread its structure and spongy crumb.

When glutenous foods enter your intestines, enzymes start breaking down the gluten into gliadin and glutenin proteins. Those who can digest gluten will absorb the proteins, but for those who can't, one of the proteins—gliadin—will be identified as dangerous and the body will produce antibodies to attack it. Over time, this results in reduced nutrient absorption and damage to the intestinal lining, which causes digestive issues, including bloating, diarrhea, eczema, and malnutrition.

What Replaces Gluten in Gluten-Free Breads?

When I first started baking gluten-free, my bread was crumbly and dry. One failure after another led me to realize that in order to replace gluten, I needed an ingredient that could replicate its binding power. Here are my three preferred binders:

EGGS

Naturally gluten-free, eggs are a great binder and leavening agent. Egg whites, which are high in protein, provide not only moisture but also a tender, light crumb. That's because beating egg whites produces air bubbles that expand inside gluten-free dough during baking. As their proteins set in the oven, eggs provide a tender, strong structure that mimics gluten.

PSYLLIUM HUSK

The most recent binder to enter the gluten-free baking scene—and revolutionize bread making—is psyllium husk, a fiber from the seeds of the *Plantago ovata* plant family. Psyllium husk is hydrophilic, meaning it attracts and binds to liquid, forming a gel and increasing dough volume much like xanthan gum does. What makes psyllium husk so valuable in gluten-free bread baking is its ability to act as a sponge, swelling as it absorbs liquid. The result is a soft dough that can be handled and shaped exactly like glutenous bread dough.

XANTHAN GUM

A binder I've used for more than a decade, xanthan gum is derived from corn. When combined with liquid, it forms a gel-like emulsion that traps bubbles incorporated during the mixing of the dough, resulting in greater aeration. This emulsifier also increases the maximum dough volume during proofing, building dough strength and elasticity while increasing loaf volume.

Bonus Health Benefits of Gluten-Free Bread

While not all gluten-free bread is "healthy" (looking at you, Triple Berry Cream Cheese Danishes, page 98), there are some inherent health benefits to using gluten-free ingredients. The blends I created for Whole-Grain Flour (page 33) and High-Protein Flour (page 32) are nutrient dense and rich in fiber, which can lower cholesterol and help maintain a healthy gastrointestinal system. And, speaking of digestion, naturally occurring bacteria developed during the fermentation of bread dough (especially sourdough) before baking helps break down the flours and starches, making it easier to digest.

Bread Baking Terms to Know

These terms help explain what's happening inside your bread dough.

Crumb: The crumb refers to the texture of the interior of a loaf of bread that can be described as a pattern of holes, determined by the gas bubbles produced during the proofing stage. For enriched doughs, such as brioche, this crumb structure resembles small, uniform holes. For artisan and sourdough bread, the holes are larger and less uniform.

Fermentation: This is the leavening process after the bread starter and remaining dough ingredients are combined and the proofing stage begins, allowing the yeast to grow, which expands the bread dough. A **long fermentation** refers to a slow rise of bread dough in the refrigerator, which slows down the fermentation process. This allows enzymes in the flours to break down the starches into sugars, which adds flavor and promotes browning in the oven. You'll see the option to use a long fermentation in most of the recipes in chapter 6 (page 103).

Sponge: Enriched breads, such as Brioche Loaf Bread (page 82), have extra ingredients (butter, milk, sugar, and eggs) that can make it challenging for fermentation to occur. That's why these recipes begin with a sponge, a type of quick dough starter. The sponge gives the yeast a head start to hydrate before the remaining ingredients are mixed in.

Starter: A traditional sourdough starter is a natural leavening agent and one of the oldest techniques used to make bread. Typically, a starter consists of a liquid made by mixing together flour and water, then letting it ferment in a warm environment (ideally 75°F). With the goal of building up the concentration of yeast, this live culture needs to be fed twice a day with flour and water over a six-day period before use for optimal results. In this cookbook, I mostly use a starter called a **poolish**, a liquidy pre-ferment (pre-fermentation) starter made of equal parts flour and water by weight along with a small amount of yeast. The starter is mixed in advance of dough preparation—at least 12 hours and up to overnight—then incorporated into the bread dough, speeding up fermentation of the finished loaf while adding flavor and structure.

What to Expect from Gluten-Free Bread

When you ditch gluten, you ditch the rules of traditional baking, too—and that's a good thing. Though your dough might not look like you'd expect, you can still create gluten-free breads of all shapes, textures, and flavors—from a seemingly impossible Brioche Loaf Bread (page 82) to Asiago Sourdough Ciabatta (page 113) to Cranberry-Pecan Sourdough Rolls (page 108). Here's what you can expect to encounter with gluten-free bread baking:

More like Batter than Dough

In the beginning of my gluten-free bread baking journey, the standard was something called a "batter bread," named because it was similar to the consistency of pancake batter before it went into the oven. The mixing process and resulting bread only vaguely resembled traditional bread doughs. There was no shaping, just pouring. However, as more gluten-free grains, starches, and binders have become available, the gluten-free baking world has changed. In this cookbook, you'll be making some bread dough that you can scoop (this type has more liquid and less flour) and some that's freestanding (more flour, less water), meaning it can hold its shape without the help of a baking pan.

No Need to Knead

Traditionally, you knead bread dough and let it proof (often several times throughout a single recipe) with the goal of developing strands of gluten. No gluten means no kneading. It's that simple!

One Rise and Done

Since we're not kneading the dough to develop gluten, there's no need to let the dough proof more than once. In gluten-free bread baking, you create rise by mixing the dough at a high speed and letting the yeast or starter build air bubbles during proofing, both of which produce a final loaf with a lighter, more open crumb. If you were to knead and fold a gluten-free bread dough after the first rise, you would lose all the aeration you developed earlier.

Final Texture and Taste

Just like traditional bread, the texture of gluten-free bread depends on the type of bread you're making—from a deliciously dense rustic loaf to an enriched bread made airy with butter and eggs. Whole grains also affect texture, similar to how glutenous whole-wheat bread is typically heavier than fluffy white bread. As for taste, gluten-free bread uses a combination of naturally gluten-free flours and starches that offer not only improved dough performance but also distinct flavors. My absolute favorite gluten-free flour is millet, which has an almost buttery flavor and a similar protein structure to wheat.

A Step-by-Step Guide to Gluten-Free Bread

Let me take you through how to make a basic gluten-free bread—from ingredient prep to finished loaf. Once you make your first loaf of bread, you'll understand just how easy the process is and that active time is minimal.

Ready Your Gluten-Free Flour Blends

Gluten-free bread baking requires a flour blend with specific ingredients that increase dough performance and the chances of successful outcomes, including flavor and texture. These are the things I thought about when creating my bread flour blends, so I highly recommend making a big batch of them in advance to have them on hand whenever you want to make bread. Store the flour blends in an airtight container and keep them in a cool, dry place or refrigerate them for up to six months.

Prep and Weigh Your Ingredients

If you've baked before, you're probably used to measuring by volume (a.k.a. using measuring cups). That changes now. Gluten-free flours and starches are especially susceptible to volume-measuring mistakes because, while they might take up the same amount of space in a measuring cup, they often have vastly different weights. For instance, 1 cup of millet flour weighs 160 grams, while 1 cup of potato starch weighs 192 grams. That's the kind of difference that can ruin a loaf of bread. The solution? Use a scale, which is undoubtedly the most accurate way to measure. Weighing your ingredients in grams promises consistency, ensuring you recreate the recipe the same way each time, with the exact amount of each ingredient you need. **That's why the measurements in this book are listed in grams, not cups.**

If you're new to weighing ingredients, start by keeping one large mixing bowl on the counter and a separate, smaller bowl on the scale to weigh each ingredient. Then follow these steps:

1. Turn on the scale.

2. Press the unit option button to set the scale to measure in grams.

3. Place the smaller mixing bowl on the scale.

4. Press the tare button to zero out the weight. The scale will read 0g.

5. Add your first ingredient to the bowl until you reach the desired weight, then transfer the ingredient to the larger mixing bowl.

6. Set the smaller bowl back on the scale and press the tare button to zero out the weight again. The scale will read 0g.

7. Weigh the next ingredient and transfer to the larger bowl. Continue weighing and taring until all ingredients are weighed.

Once you're comfortable with the weighing process, you can start measuring multiple ingredients in one bowl. Set a large mixing bowl on the scale and follow the instructions. Skip the step in which you transfer each ingredient after weighing and simply hit the tare button instead. This will zero out the weight of the bowl and the previous ingredient(s).

IMPORTANT NOTE: There are two exceptions to the always-weigh-it rule. First, unless you have a highly precise scale, weighing any ingredient under 10 grams can be tricky. In the upcoming recipes, I've provided a measuring spoon equivalent in parentheses for these tiny measurements. The margin of error between weight and volume is small enough in these instances that it won't affect the outcome of your bread. Second, some recipes have non-bread elements (such as dip or filling) that don't need to be measured in grams because they don't go into the dough itself. I've provided you both grams and cups measurements for these ingredients—feel free to use the method that suits you.

Mix Your Dough

An advantage of gluten-free bread dough is that there's no need to worry about overmixing the dough and therefore overdeveloping the gluten, which would result in a tough loaf of bread. To mix, you can use a large mixing bowl and dough whisk (for more about this tool, see page 24) or a stand mixer fitted with the paddle attachment. After all the ingredients are combined, I increase the speed on the stand mixer to medium and beat the dough for three minutes to add air to the dough and hydrate the flours, which builds in air pockets that create light, fluffy bread.

Shape and Proof

Shaping gluten-free bread dough is easy. In this cookbook, you'll transfer your mixed dough into a loaf pan, into a proofing basket, or onto a piece of parchment paper, then use a wet offset spatula (for more about this tool, see page 25) or spoon to gently smooth out the surface. That's it! The shaping process couldn't be simpler. To proof the dough, you'll cover the surface of the dough loosely with plastic wrap to keep it from creating a crust, then let the dough proof at room temperature until puffy, usually about 1½ hours. For some of the enriched and sourdough bread recipes, you'll transfer the shaped dough to the refrigerator and proof for about 10 hours or overnight to let it slowly ferment and develop a complex flavor (this is the long fermentation technique mentioned earlier).

Score and Bake

After you proof your bread dough (and let it return to room temperature, if you chose a long fermentation), you may want to score it. Scoring is the process of slashing the surface of the dough to allow for maximum expansion during baking without tearing and cracking, and it can be straightforward or decorative. To score your dough, you'll need a lame (for more about this tool, see page 24), single-edge razor blade, or sharp paring knife. Without hesitation, run the blade across the surface of the dough, creating a cut about ¼ inch deep. In the beginning, you may want to start simple with a single straight score, a crosshatch design, or leaf shape (below). As you get more comfortable slashing bread dough, your patterns can get more elaborate.

When it comes time to bake, you'll use my secret trick for even, crispy bread: turn a rimmed baking sheet upside down and place it in the oven before you preheat (the upside down placement lifts the dough off the oven rack to increase air flow). You could also use a clay pizza stone or baking steel.. All of these tools absorb, retain, and radiate heat, so when you place the dough on top to bake, you'll get an evenly baked bread with a crispy crust. This technique also gives dough an initial burst of heat to help it rise. My other trick for a no-fail golden, crackling crust? Parchment paper bags, which simulate professional bread ovens by trapping steam while baking.

Cool and Store

Cooling is a critical part of the bread baking process. Most recipes call for letting the loaf cool completely on a wire rack before slicing. The reason is twofold: (1) the flavor continues to develop as the bread rests, and (2) the moisture rises to the crust and evaporates during this time. If you cut or tear the bread while it's cooling, the moisture will still be in the center of the bread, making the crumb gummy and damp. Generally, a cooled loaf can be stored in a sealed paper bag for up to two days or frozen in a resealable freezer bag for up to one month. While enriched breads like brioche are best fresh, you can slice and refrigerate or freeze for later use in French toast, bread pudding, or even stuffing.

Tips for Gluten-Free Success

Now that you have a step-by-step understanding of how the gluten-free bread baking process works, it's time for me to share my no-fail tips for making tasty, showstopping bread you'll love.

Temperature Matters

As with any type of baking, temperature is important and affects the outcome of your gluten-free bread. In bread baking specifically, when you're working with yeast and starter, the speed at which yeast grows and dough ferments depends on the temperature of both the ingredients and your kitchen. There are three stages of bread making where temperature can impact your loaf: mixing, proofing, and baking. For mixing, the ideal kitchen temperature is 75°F to 78°F. For proofing, anywhere from 75°F to 95°F, with 81°F being optimal (see A Trick for Proofing Dough, page 15). And for baking, depending on whether the dough is enriched or not, 350°F and up is best. As for liquid ingredients, the ideal temperature for lukewarm water is about 65°F and for milk it's about 100°F. A food thermometer is a good tool to measure temperature, even when it comes to a recipe requiring room-temperature ingredients, like butter, which is ideal for easily blending into dough at about 68°F.

Make Sure Your Yeast Is Active

This cookbook calls for instant yeast, which was developed to be added directly to dry ingredients and is 100 percent active right from the package. I recommend checking the expiration date before use, because dead yeast means bread that won't rise. To test your yeast, stir together a packet of instant yeast with ½ teaspoon of sugar in a small bowl, then stir in ½ cup of warm water and wait 10 minutes to see if the yeast is bubbling, a visual cue that it's active. If it does not bubble or foam, discard it and start over with new yeast.

Start with a Higher-Protein Flour Blend

The amount of protein in flour yields different crumb structures. Flours with less protein will result in a light, fluffy crumb, while flours with higher protein levels result in a chewy crumb. That's why different types of flour exist for different baked goods: cake flour is 9 percent protein, all-purpose is 10 percent, and bread flour is 12 percent. For my High-Protein Flour (page 32), I chose specific protein-rich ingredients to replicate the levels found in traditional glutenous bread flour. Millet, the flour I prefer, has 4 grams of protein per ¼ cup. To add more protein, I also incorporate organic sprouted brown rice protein powder (32 grams of protein per ¼ cup) and golden flaxseed meal (6 grams of protein per ¼ cup).

Avoid Over- or Under-Proofing

Like with traditional bread, under- or over-proofing gluten-free bread dough can result in inconsistent crumb structure or a sunken loaf. Over-proofing means the dough rested for too long after mixing and shaping, or your kitchen was too warm and the yeast grew too quickly. When you put over-proofed dough into the oven, it has no more expanding left to do because the air bubbles inside of it have popped, creating a loss of dough structure and a gummy interior. Under-proofing is the exact opposite—meaning the dough didn't rest for long enough and didn't create enough gas bubbles before it went into the oven, creating a loaf with little rise and a dense crumb.

A TRICK FOR PROOFING DOUGH: If you don't have a proof setting on your oven, here's one method I've used to create a moist, warm environment for rising bread dough: Preheat your oven to 200°F, then let it heat for two minutes. Turn off the oven and carefully place a bowl of boiling water on the bottom rack. Place the covered, shaped bread dough on the center rack, close the oven door, and proof. (Note: You can use this method any time the recipes call for proofing dough at room temperature. It's especially helpful in the wintertime when "room temperature" is too cold for optimal proofing.)

Boost Flavor with a Bread Starter, Soaked Grains, or Both

Want more flavor? My secret is bread starter, which gives bread more acidity, which equates to better structure and flavor. I also love soaking grains to add flavor and texture to a finished loaf. When you soak grains before mixing them into a bread dough, the grains hydrate, absorbing water and softening as opposed to absorbing the water in the bread dough, which would yield a dry loaf with undercooked grains. You'll see this technique used throughout the recipes in chapter 3.

Troubleshooting Gluten-Free Breads

Bread baking is a process of patience and learning about your environment. Professional bakers prepare their dough based on several factors, including the humidity and temperature levels where the dough will be rising. Then they adjust the amount of yeast, sourdough starter, and water they use. Inevitably, you will run into some challenges as you get started, but don't let them discourage you. Many of the most common problems have simple solutions.

Look at these issues as learning tools that only make your bread better, loaf after loaf.

General Questions

Why isn't my bread dough rising?

Yeast production (what makes your dough rise) is very environment dependent. Make sure your dough is rising in a warm, humid area of your kitchen. Try the method explained in A Trick for Proofing Dough (page 15).

Why is my loaf gummy and wet on the inside?

Gummy, wet dough is usually the result of too much or too little hydration. Flours absorb water at different rates. The fresher the flour, the more water it absorbs. I recommend reducing the total amount of liquid by 30 grams at the start of the recipe. If you have already mixed a dough and see that it's too wet, add more flour blend 30 grams at a time. If you're using a store-bought gluten-free flour blend, that could also be the reason.

Why is my bread dense and heavy?

Heavy, dense bread can happen when the dough is not mixed long enough to create aeration. Using a stand mixer is more consistent than mixing by hand. Also, your oven may not have been properly preheated, reducing the likelihood of oven spring (the rise caused by the burst of heat that hits the dough during the first few minutes of heat). Another possibility is that your ingredient measurements may be off—this is more likely if you converted the grams measurements to measuring cups instead of using a scale (see Prep and Weigh Your Ingredients, page 8).

Why did my loaf deflate when it came out of the oven?

This can happen if the dough is underbaked and the internal structure isn't solid enough. Browning means flavor, so don't be tempted to remove your loaf from the oven early. If you feel like the crust is getting too dark, cover the top loosely with aluminum foil and continue baking.

What ingredients can I use to replace the dairy in the recipes?

Thankfully, there are now many options available at the supermarket that you can swap in for the dairy ingredients in the recipes. See the Substitution Cheat Sheet (page 30) for dairy alternatives you can use in this book's recipes. You can also make your own dairy-free milks and cheeses using my cookbook, *Silvana's Gluten-Free and Dairy-Free Kitchen*.

Are your bread recipes egg-free? Can I use an egg replacer?

Most of my recipes contain eggs, especially egg whites. I have not tested these recipes with egg replacers and can't guarantee they will yield similar results.

Can I freeze raw bread dough?

Instead of freezing raw dough, I recommend baking your loaf, then slicing and freezing the bread for later. You can thaw the bread at room temperature or in the refrigerator.

Enriched Doughs

Why is the inside of my enriched bread raw?

It's possible that your oven temperature was too high, causing the crust to brown too fast without cooking the interior. Or, maybe the loaf didn't cool completely and the moisture got trapped inside (see Cool and Store, page 13).

Why didn't my enriched dough rise?

The milk may have been too hot and killed the enzymes in the yeast, or it could have been too cold and slowed down the rising time. Place the dough in a warm, humid environment to see if that helps. Use a thermometer to measure liquid temperatures in future recipes.

Pre-Ferments and Sourdough

How do I know when my pre-ferment or sourdough starter is becoming active?

You'll begin to see some bubbles and the starter rising in the jar. This means the yeast is feeding, growing and producing carbon dioxide. Use an elastic or piece of masking tape to mark the level of the starter after each feeding to see how your starter is progressing. Under the right temperature, humidity, and feeding schedule, the starter should visibly rise in the jar.

How can I get a more open crumb?

Feeding the starter twice a day (morning and evening or about 12 hours apart) as opposed to once a day will make it more active (and reduce bacteria), resulting in a more open crumb. See the instructions on page 19 on maintaining a sourdough starter.

How to Start (and Keep) a Sourdough Starter

The recipes in chapter 6 (page 103) begin with instructions for making a quick version of a gluten-free starter called a poolish, but if you'd rather maintain an active gluten-free sourdough starter, here's my step-by-step guide. You can use it in all recipes that call for a starter and save yourself a ton of time (simply skip step 1 in those recipes).

For this starter, I chose millet flour because of its flavor. Once you're in starter maintenance mode, you can either continue using millet flour, use a combination of millet flour and another gluten-free flour (such as brown rice, oat, or sorghum flour), or switch out the millet flour completely with one or more gluten-free flours.

DAY 1: MAKE THE STARTER

Raw honey, a concentrated source of natural sugar that contains wild yeast, helps jump-start the starter. If you use a dish towel to cover your starter, use a flour sack one, which is more breathable. To encourage your starter to grow, place it in a warm environment, such as your kitchen counter near the stove. (Don't use A Trick for Proofing Dough, page 15, here. That could cause your starter to overflow.)

Initial Mixture
295g water at 75°F
280g millet flour
7g (1 teaspoon) raw honey

Pour the water into a 1½-quart glass jar. Add the millet flour and honey; stir to combine, scraping down the sides if necessary. Cover with cheesecloth or a clean dish towel; let it sit in a warm place at room temperature for about 24 hours.

DAY 2: BUILD THE STARTER

Your starter isn't active yet, so it won't be bubbly. Now, you'll begin feeding the starter using a portion of the ripened starter from yesterday (and discarding the rest) to encourage the wild yeast to grow. You'll do this in both the morning and evening to reduce bacteria and build more active yeast, resulting in a more open crumb when you use it in a bread recipe.

Morning Feed

240g water at 70°F

200g ripened starter

320g millet flour

Pour the water into a clean 1½-quart glass jar. Add the ripened starter and flour; stir to combine, scraping down the sides if necessary. Cover with cheese-cloth or a clean dish towel; let it sit in a warm place at room temperature for about 12 hours.

Evening Feed

120g water at 70°F

100g ripened starter

160g millet flour

Pour the water into a clean 1½-quart glass jar. Add the ripened starter and flour; stir to combine, scraping down the sides if necessary. Cover with cheese-cloth or a clean dish towel; let it sit in a warm place at room temperature for about 12 hours.

DAYS 3 TO 5

Repeat morning and evening feedings using the measurements above. At this point in the process, your starter will be more active, growing and producing carbon dioxide. You'll begin to see some bubbles as the starter rises in the jar.

DAY 6

Your starter should now be ready to use or maintain. Store either at room temperature if you want to use it right away, or in the refrigerator if you plan to use it later. If you just fed your starter and plan to refrigerate it, let it sit at room temperature for 6 hours before storing it in the refrigerator.

DAY 7+

You'll use cooler water to maintain your starter from now on, which slows down fermentation while building acidity and flavor.

FOR REGULAR USE

Feed your starter daily in the morning and evening if you plan to bake with it regularly.

Morning and Evening Feedings

75g water at 60°F
75g ripened starter
75g millet flour

Place the water In a clean 1½-quart glass jar. Add the ripened starter and flour; stir to combine, scraping down the sides if necessary. Cover with cheesecloth or a clean dish towel; let it sit in a warm place at room temperature for about 12 hours. (If you just fed your starter, let it sit at room temperature for 6 hours before using it in a recipe.)

FOR LATER USE

If you're not actively using your starter but want to keep it alive, store it in the refrigerator and feed it weekly. Bring the starter to room temperature before each feeding. When you're ready to use the starter in a recipe, resume daily morning and evening feedings for at least one day, or until you begin to see bubbles again.

Weekly Maintenance Feedings

75g water at 60°F
75g ripened starter
75g millet flour

Place the water in a clean 1½-quart glass jar. Add the ripened starter and flour; stir to combine, scraping down the sides if necessary. Cover with cheesecloth or a clean dish towel; let it sit in a warm place at room temperature for about 12 hours, then transfer it back to the refrigerator after using it in your recipe.

CHAPTER 2

PREPARING TO BAKE

In this chapter, I'll detail the everyday kitchen tools I rely on, as well as my three favorite flour blends for gluten-free bread baking success. Stock your kitchen, then let's start baking!

A Bread Baker's Tools

If you've done any baking in the past, you'll likely already have most of the items on this list in your kitchen. Some tools are critical and others are optional—although they can make bread baking easier and more successful while saving you time. I'll call out the optional items in the list that follows.

ALUMINUM BAKING SHEETS: I use rimmed, 12-gauge, 18-by-13-inch commercial baking sheets, which conduct heat evenly and don't buckle under high temperatures used for baking bread.

DIGITAL SCALE: This is the most essential tool for a baker. I've had my digital scale since 2004 and have used it almost every day for all my baking needs. See Prep and Weigh Your Ingredients (page 8) for why it's so critical. You'll want a scale that has a tare feature and weighs in grams.

DOUGH WHISK: Also called a Danish dough whisk, this tool doesn't look like the standard balloon whisk you might be imagining. It consists of three various-size coils designed to work through dough without overmixing or getting stuck like a balloon whisk would. If you don't have a stand mixer, you'll definitely want to invest in one of these before you start on your gluten-free bread baking journey.

LAME OR SINGLE-EDGE RAZOR BLADE: I use a lame to score the surface of the dough before baking, allowing for rapid expansion of the dough in the oven. You could also use a single-edge razor blade or sharp paring knife.

LOAF PANS: Some breads need structure, especially sandwich breads, which require a specific height. I've been using 5-by-9-inch cast-iron loaf pans for more than a decade. They absorb, retain, and distribute heat evenly. You can also use standard metal loaf pans in the same size.

MIXING BOWLS: Any bowls will do, but I prefer my nested stainless-steel set, which is ideal for mixing small or large amounts of ingredients. They're also lightweight, which is helpful when using a scale.

OFFSET SERRATED BREAD KNIFE: I use this to slice baked bread. Because it's offset, it's easier to slice all the way to the bottom and make slices an even width. You can also use a standard serrated knife.

OFFSET SPATULA: This is my tool of choice for shaping and smoothing free-standing bread dough. When you wet it slightly with water and run it along the top and sides of the dough, it creates a beautifully smooth finish. An offset spatula is a versatile baking tool that you won't mind keeping around (it's great for icing cakes), but you can use a spoon in its place.

OVEN AND FOOD THERMOMETERS: It's critical to know you're baking at the right temperature. I always keep an oven thermometer in my oven to double check. You also may find a food thermometer helpful to ensure your liquid ingredients are at the right temperature (which can impact how well your yeast performs).

PARCHMENT PAPER AND PLASTIC WRAP: I've been using parchment paper since I opened my bakery back in 2004—and I've never looked back. I never have to worry about anything sticking to the baking pan, plus it makes for fast and easy cleanup. As far as plastic wrap, this will be your go-to for covering dough while it proofs.

PARCHMENT PAPER COOKING BAGS: These bags have been a game changer for baking gluten-free bread. They create a sealed, moist heat environment, delivering a deep golden, crackling crust thanks to the steam that builds and gets trapped inside while baking. You can make your own bags from standard parchment paper, but it's time-consuming and not worth the hassle. Parchment paper bags are inexpensive and readily available online. I recommend the If You Care brand.

PASTRY BRUSH: In bread baking, you'll use a pastry brush to gently apply an even coat of egg wash or melted jam onto enriched breads and danishes, giving them a golden color and sheen. You can also use it to brush away excess flour from dough or parchment paper. There's no good alternative for a pastry brush, so you'll want to invest in one (or several).

PROOFING BASKET: Also known as a *banneton* or *brotform*, a proofing basket—made of coiled natural cane—helps bread dough rise evenly and maintain its shape during the proofing process while giving the dough its signature spiral indentations. Sometimes, I like to line the basket with a thin potato sack dish towel for a smoother exterior finish. A proofing basket is an optional tool.

RUBBER SPATULA OR BOWL SCRAPER: I use both rubber spatulas and a bowl scraper to clean my mixing bowls of any remaining dough. Either will work!

SPRAY BOTTLE: I like to spritz bread dough before baking (and sometimes halfway through baking) to create steam and, ultimately, a nice crispy crust. You don't need a spray bottle to do this, but it helps.

STAND MIXER: While not necessary, a stand mixer will definitely save you some elbow grease and time. When it comes to gluten-free bread baking, you'll be using the paddle—not the dough hook—attachment to mix and aerate the dough.

WIRE COOLING RACKS: These are essential to properly cool any baked good. You'll place your baking pans hot out of the oven directly on the wire racks and, for most bread recipes, let the bread cool completely. Be sure to purchase a set—you'll need more than one, and they'll come in handy for anything you bake.

Your Gluten-Free Bread Pantry

I've done all the ingredient testing to achieve the best outcomes for gluten-free bread so you don't have to. Here are the essential ingredients you need to bake the recipes in this cookbook. I've also included a Substitution Cheat Sheet on page 30 for easy ingredient swaps, especially dairy-free ideas for those of you who are avoiding or intolerant to dairy.

Starches and Flours

Without a specific blend of starches and flours, it would be impossible to achieve any baked good, bread included. Here are my favorites for performance and flavor.

CORNSTARCH: The lighter the flour blend, the lighter the loaf, and cornstarch is the lightest of all starches. That's why I use it as the predominant starch in my whole-grain and high-protein bread blends, yielding the best results.

MILLET FLOUR: My favorite flour for its neutral buttery-sweet flavor, millet is a nutritious, protein-rich seeded grass that gives structure to bread dough.

POTATO STARCH: Not to be confused with potato flour, potato starch (in combination with other starches like cornstarch and tapioca flour) helps yield a lighter loaf.

TAPIOCA FLOUR: Lighter than potato starch, tapioca flour (also known as tapioca starch) is an extract from cassava root. It's the secret to my All-Purpose Flour blend (page 31), making for gluten-free baked goods that yield the same texture as their glutenous counterparts.

WHITE RICE FLOUR: This flour is one of the ingredients in my All-Purpose Flour blend (page 31), which I combine with tapioca flour, potato starch, salt, and xanthan gum. While you can substitute whole-grain brown rice flour for more nutrition, it results in denser breads.

Binders and Thickeners

While binders and thickeners help build the structure of bread, I rely on them most for their ability to give gluten-free flours and starches elasticity. I've already mentioned xanthan gum and psyllium husk (see What Replaces Gluten in Gluten-Free Breads?, page 4), but there's one more you should know about.

GOLDEN FLAXSEED MEAL: Like psyllium husk powder and xanthan gum, fiber-rich flaxseed meal adds body and structure to bread dough while giving bread a wonderful nuttiness.

Salt

In my kitchen, I use fine sea salt for baking, which dissolves in liquid easily. If you're weighing salt for a recipe, you can use any salt you have on hand. If you're using measuring spoons, make sure your salt is fine, not coarse.

Yeast

I prefer using instant yeast because you can mix it directly into dry ingredients. Active dry yeast requires blooming before it can be used in a recipe, meaning you first need to rehydrate/activate the yeast in warm water with sugar and wait 5 to 10 minutes for it to froth before using. This makes instant yeast super convenient, especially when prepping a large quantity of gluten-free bread blends for multiple uses. Instant yeast also saves time by eliminating the blooming step.

Eggs, Fats, and Milks

I use eggs, fats (such as butter), and milk to enrich some of my bread recipes, tenderizing the dough.

BUTTER: I use unsalted butter, which results in a rich, moist bread texture while adding a faint grassy sweetness to the dough.

BUTTERMILK AND YOGURT: While buttermilk and yogurt add a slight tang to bread, I use them for their acidic properties to give bread dough a boost while it proofs and create a lighter texture in the finished loaf.

EGGS: While eggs provide color, I use them more as a leavening agent, giving gluten-free bread a nice spring in the oven. The recipes in this cookbook call for large eggs. Any other size egg will not yield the same results.

MILK: Because milk increases absorption more than water, it gives bread a softer and lighter texture. It also slows down fermentation, which translates into a more flavorful loaf (enzymes in the yeast start breaking down starch into sugar, producing carbon dioxide and alcohol along with acetic acid and amino acid, resulting in a more complex flavor profile). I use whole milk for its full fat content, which is a tenderizer.

Sweeteners

In most of my bread recipes, I use some sort of sweetener.

GRANULATED SUGAR: This plays several roles in bread making. Sugar feeds the yeast, helping the dough rise by converting sugar to carbon dioxide and alcohol. It also enhances browning when the bread is baking, as sugar rises to the surface of the dough.

HONEY: I use raw honey for sourdough starter to jump-start the naturally occurring yeast production in flour. It also adds flavor and browning to finished baked goods.

Flavor Boosts

These extra ingredients aren't integral to bread baking, but they do take your loaves from good to absolutely delicious.

CHEESE: There's no doubt cheese adds flavor and texture to anything, including bread. In this cookbook, I incorporate Asiago, Gorgonzola, Parmesan, and cream cheese into savory and sweet doughs. Unless I'm creaming the cheese into a dough, I add crumbled or shredded cheese at the end of the mixing process so the pieces stay mostly intact, creating melted pockets of cheese in baked breads.

CHOCOLATE: Because everything tastes better with chocolate—especially bread. I prefer using semisweet chocolate, but any chocolate works well.

DRIED FRUITS: I like to add a burst of flavor to my bread by using dried fruits, such as cranberries and sun-dried tomatoes. I prefer unsweetened dried fruit, but you can use whatever you have on hand.

FRESH HERBS: I've always incorporated fresh herbs into recipes because they add flavor to anything I make. You can really add any herb. A few of my favorites include chopped rosemary, parsley, basil, and cilantro.

SEEDS: There are so many to choose from—think sesame, poppy, sunflower, caraway, and fennel. They all add a unique crunch to the finished loaf. If you toast them before adding them to bread dough, you'll bring out a wonderfully nutty flavor.

SPICES: Seasonings, such as buffalo wing seasoning, everything bagel seasoning, and Italian seasoning create fun flavor-specific breads. Go ahead and play with your favorite seasonings.

SUBSTITUTION CHEAT SHEET

INGREDIENT	SUBSTITUTIONS	CONSIDERATIONS
Buttermilk	Make your own by combining 240 grams (1 cup) dairy-free milk with 14.5 grams (1 tablespoon) apple cider vinegar	Let the mixture stand for 10 minutes to allow it to activate. Store in the refrigerator in a resealable container for up to 3 days.
Cheese	Dairy-free store-bought cheese or homemade dairy-free cheese from *Silvana's Gluten-Free and Dairy-Free Kitchen*	There are plenty of great meltable dairy-free cheese options on the market these days. You can also make them yourself (or omit cheese entirely from a recipe).
Unsalted butter	Nonhydrogenated shortening or dairy-free buttery sticks	If the recipe calls for room-temperature butter, you can use shortening or buttery sticks made for baking (not spreading). If the recipe calls for melted butter, you can use melted shortening, buttery sticks, or a neutral-flavored oil, such as sunflower seed.
Whole milk	Unsweetened dairy-free milk or water	You can use any home-made unsweetened dairy-free milk or a store-bought one, prefer-ably without stabilizers or emulsifiers (such as guar gum, xanthan gum, acacia gum, carrageenan, and locust bean gum). In a pinch, you can also use water.

The Only Gluten-Free Flour Blends You'll Need

I've spent more than a decade developing these three flour blends—a general all-purpose, whole-grain, and high-protein blend. You can use the All-Purpose Flour for all of your baking needs and the Whole-Grain and High-Protein Flours for any yeasted baked goods. They keep for up to six months when stored in a cool, dry place (like your pantry) or the refrigerator.

ALL-PURPOSE FLOUR

YIELD: About 10 cups

Having tested countless store-bought flour mixes, I can humbly report that mine continuously outperforms the others in terms of flavor and texture. My blend is a mix of white starches, but if you want more fiber, you can swap half the white rice flour for brown rice flour.

870g white rice flour

375g tapioca flour

246g potato starch

18g xanthan gum

9g (1 tablespoon) salt

In a large bowl, whisk together all the ingredients. Transfer to an airtight storage container.

HIGH-PROTEIN FLOUR

YIELD: About 10 cups

As I mentioned earlier, high-protein bread flour helps build structure and texture in the finished loaf. After testing several powdered proteins, I settled on raw rice protein powder, which has a neutral flavor and color. The flax-seed meal and psyllium husk powder also add body and stability.

480g cornstarch

270g potato starch

240g white rice flour

210g millet flour

159g golden flaxseed meal

90g granulated sugar

81g raw rice protein powder

54g psyllium husk powder

27g salt

26.25g (three ¼-ounce packages) instant yeast

9g (1 tablespoon) xanthan gum

In a large bowl, whisk together all the ingredients. Transfer to an airtight storage container.

WHOLE-GRAIN FLOUR

YIELD: About 10 cups

This recipe uses brown rice flour and millet flour, two fiber- and protein-rich whole grains. As with glutenous whole-grain flours, it's heavier than all-purpose flour. If you want to lighten it up, swap in white rice flour for the brown rice flour.

630g cornstarch

360g potato starch

315g brown rice flour

210g millet flour

54g psyllium husk powder

30g salt

26.25g (three ¼-ounce packages) instant yeast

18g granulated sugar

9g (1 tablespoon) xanthan gum

In a large bowl, whisk together all the ingredients. Transfer to an airtight storage container.

What about Store-Bought Gluten-Free Flour Blends?

Every gluten-free flour blend consists of various flours and starches in different ratios. Each ingredient contains a unique nutritional, functional, and flavor profile. I've crafted my own blends to produce the best possible breads for the recipes in this book. If you have a favorite blend or want to get started as quickly as possible, you can try a store-bought blend in these recipes; however, I can't guarantee the outcome will be as good.

How to Use the Recipes

Just the smell of baking bread is intoxicating, and taking that first bite is comforting and satisfying, especially if you've gone without or settled for less-than-satisfactory loaves on your gluten-free journey. When I started developing recipes for this book, my main goal was to go back to basics. I reexamined the bread baking essentials I've learned over the years and decided what to keep and what to leave behind to build a better gluten-free bread baking experience. I chose these recipes specifically to deliver those positive emotions only freshly-baked bread can deliver—there's nothing quite like it.

The recipes in this book include both adaptations of my favorite breads, like Fennel Raisin Semolina-Style Bread (page 50), and new recipes, like Triple Berry Cream Cheese Danishes (page 98), inspired by my brioche dough. The book is divided into four baking categories: artisanal breads, sandwich breads and pizza, enriched breads, and sourdough breads. In each recipe, I've noted whether the recipes are dairy-free, nut-free, and/or egg-free.

Recipe Tips

Before you begin a recipe, be sure to read the entire thing from start to finish so you know what's coming. Carefully review the list of ingredients and tools needed; the active, inactive, and total time commitment required; and the step-by-step instructions. The ingredients are listed in the order you'll use them. When you're ready to make a recipe, gather all the ingredients together, noting any refrigerated items that need to come to room temperature before starting.

I've also included tips at the end of most recipes to clarify instructions or provide suggestions for swapping certain ingredients.

PART 2

GLUTEN-FREE BREAD RECIPES

Get your mixing bowls ready, it's time to make some bread. In the upcoming recipes, you'll find of my favorite artisanal breads, sandwich breads and pizza, enriched breads, and sourdoughs, including Olive Herb Bread Twists (page 54), Pumpernickel-Style Bread (page 48), Garlic Butter Focaccia Bread (page 72), and Muffaletta-Style Pizza (page 78), to name a few. Let's get baking!

OLIVE HERB BREAD TWISTS, PAGE 54

CHAPTER 3

ARTISANAL BREADS

Traditionally, artisanal bread is made using only four key ingredients: flour, water, yeast, and salt. What makes them special is a return to the fundamentals of old-world bread baking, including shaping each loaf by hand.

COUNTRY BREAD

This basic bread is anything but, well, basic. It has a crusty exterior and a moist, tender interior crumb. It can be shaped into round or oval loafs or rolls. It's also my go-to base recipe to make a variety of flavored artisan breads, including pumpernickel and fennel raisin bread.

YIELD: 1 (1-pound) loaf **ACTIVE TIME:** 15 minutes
BAKE TIME: 1 hour 20 minutes **TOTAL TIME:** 3 hours 35 minutes

TOOLS NEEDED

kitchen scale

stand mixer with paddle attachment or large bowl and dough whisk

parchment paper

offset spatula or spoon

plastic wrap

rimmed baking sheet

bread lame or sharp knife

14.3-by-3.6-by-10.6-inch nonstick parchment paper cooking bag (see Tip)

heatproof clip (optional)

wire rack

INGREDIENTS

275g High-Protein Flour (page 32), plus more for dusting

3g (½ teaspoon) salt

128g lukewarm water (65°F)

2 large egg whites (60g), at room temperature, or 60g more lukewarm water (65°F)

12g sunflower seed oil

2g (½ teaspoon) apple cider vinegar

1. **COMBINE:** In a large bowl using a dough whisk or in the bowl of a stand mixer fitted with the paddle attachment, mix together the High-Protein Flour and salt on low speed. Add the water, egg whites, sunflower seed oil, and vinegar; mix until combined. Increase the speed to medium and beat for 3 minutes to add air to the dough.

2. **SHAPE:** Generously dust a piece of parchment paper with High-Protein Flour; place the dough onto the parchment paper. Using a wet offset spatula or spoon, shape the dough into a loaf and gently smooth out the surface.

3. **PROOF:** Cover the dough loosely with plastic wrap and proof at room temperature until the dough is puffy, about 1½ hours.

4. **PREHEAT:** Place an inverted rimmed baking sheet on the middle rack of the oven and preheat to 400°F. Dust the top of the dough with High-Protein Flour. Using a bread lame or sharp knife, score the surface crosswise with three diagonal lines and slide the dough on the parchment paper into a parchment paper cooking bag. Fold the bag opening several turns or use a heatproof clip to seal.

5. **BAKE:** Place the cooking bag on the preheated baking sheet and bake until the loaf is crusty and sounds hollow when tapped on the bottom, about 1 hour 20 minutes.

6. **COOL:** Carefully tear open the bag (hot steam will escape), remove the loaf, and let cool completely, about 30 minutes, on a wire rack before slicing.

TIP: The nonstick parchment paper cooking bags called for throughout the book are the medium-size bags made by a brand called If You Care. They are readily available online.

WHOLE-GRAIN BREAD

This go-to recipe is full of hearty grains, including steel-cut oats and a longtime favorite of mine, nutrient-dense millet. Besides adding a nice crunch, it gives the finished loaf an almost buttery flavor.

YIELD: 1 (1-pound) loaf **ACTIVE TIME:** 10 minutes
BAKE TIME: 1 hour 20 minutes **TOTAL TIME:** 3 hours 30 minutes

TOOLS NEEDED

kitchen scale

small bowl

stand mixer with paddle attachment or large bowl and dough whisk

parchment paper

offset spatula or spoon

plastic wrap

rimmed baking sheet

bread lame or sharp knife

14.3-by-3.6-by-10.6-inch nonstick parchment paper cooking bag (see Tip, page 41)

heatproof clip (optional)

wire rack

INGREDIENTS

44g steel-cut oats

22g hulled whole millet, plus more for sprinkling (see Tip)

20g corn grits (polenta), plus more for sprinkling

275g Whole-Grain Flour (page 33), plus more for dusting

3g (½ teaspoon) salt

128g lukewarm water (65°F)

2 large egg whites (60g), at room temperature, or 60g more lukewarm water (65°F)

12g sunflower seed oil

2g (½ teaspoon) apple cider vinegar

1. **SOAK:** Place the oats, millet, and grits in a small bowl and cover with 80g (⅓ cup) boiling water; let sit for 5 minutes, then drain well.

2. **COMBINE:** In a large bowl with a dough whisk or in the bowl of a stand mixer fitted with the paddle attachment, mix together the Whole-Grain Flour and salt on low speed. Add the lukewarm water, egg whites, sunflower seed oil, vinegar, and drained grains; mix until combined. Increase the speed to medium and beat for 3 minutes to add air to the dough.

3. **SHAPE:** Generously dust a piece of parchment paper with Whole-Grain Flour; place the dough onto the parchment paper. Using a wet offset spatula or spoon, shape the dough into a loaf and gently smooth out the surface.

4. **PROOF:** Cover the dough loosely with plastic wrap and proof at room temperature until the dough is puffy, about 1½ hours.

5. **PREHEAT:** Place an inverted rimmed baking sheet on the middle rack of the oven and preheat to 400°F. Spray the top of the dough with water and generously sprinkle with millet and cornmeal. Using a bread lame or sharp knife, score the surface in three places and slide the dough on the parchment paper into a parchment paper cooking bag; fold the bag opening several turns or use a heatproof clip to seal.

6. **BAKE:** Place the cooking bag on the preheated baking sheet and bake until the loaf is crusty and sounds hollow when tapped on the bottom, about 1 hour 20 minutes.

7. **COOL:** Carefully tear open the bag (hot steam will escape), remove the loaf, and let cool completely, about 30 minutes, on a wire rack before slicing.

TIP: No whole millet? Use sorghum or quinoa instead.

SEEDED MULTI-GRAIN ROLLS

Warm out of the oven and smothered with salted butter, these bread rolls are perfect for dinner or an afternoon snack. They have a crusty exterior and added crunch on the inside from the sunflower seeds, flaxseed, and sesame seeds.

YIELD: 4 (4-ounce) rolls **ACTIVE TIME:** 10 minutes
BAKE TIME: 35 minutes **TOTAL TIME:** 2 hours 35 minutes

TOOLS NEEDED

kitchen scale

small bowl

stand mixer with paddle attachment or large bowl and dough whisk

parchment paper

3-ounce ice cream scoop or ⅓ cup measuring cup

offset spatula or spoon

plastic wrap

rimmed baking sheet

14.3-by-3.6-by-10.6-inch nonstick parchment paper cooking bag

heatproof clip (optional)

wire rack

INGREDIENTS

35g raw sunflower seeds, plus more for sprinkling

20g flaxseed, plus more for sprinkling

20g sesame seeds, plus more for sprinkling

275g Whole-Grain Flour (page 33), plus more for dusting

3g (½ teaspoon) salt

128g lukewarm water (65°F)

2 large egg whites (60g), at room temperature, or 60g more lukewarm water (65°F)

12g sunflower seed oil

2g (½ teaspoon) apple cider vinegar

1. **SOAK:** Place the sunflower seeds, flaxseed, and sesame seeds in a small bowl and cover with 80g (⅓ cup) boiling water; let sit for 5 minutes, then drain well.

2. **COMBINE:** In a large bowl with a dough whisk or in the bowl of a stand mixer fitted with the paddle attachment, mix together the Whole-Grain Flour and salt on low speed. Add the lukewarm water, egg whites, sunflower seed oil, vinegar, and drained grains; mix until combined. Increase the speed to medium and beat for 3 minutes to add air to the dough.

3. **SHAPE:** Generously dust a piece of parchment paper with Whole-Grain Flour; using a wet 3-ounce ice cream scoop or ⅓ cup, scoop the dough onto the parchment paper, spacing the rolls about 2 inches apart. Using a wet offset spatula or spoon, gently smooth out the surface of each roll.

4. **PROOF:** Cover loosely with plastic wrap and proof at room temperature until the dough is puffy, about 1½ hours.

5. **PREHEAT:** Place an inverted rimmed baking sheet on the middle rack of the oven and preheat to 400°F. Dust the top of the rolls with Whole-Grain Flour and slide the dough on the parchment paper into a parchment paper cooking bag; fold the bag opening several turns or use a heatproof clip to seal.

6. **BAKE:** Place the cooking bag on the preheated baking sheet and bake until the rolls are crusty and sound hollow when tapped on the bottom, about 35 minutes.

7. **COOL:** Carefully tear open the bag (hot steam will escape), remove the loaf, and let cool completely, about 20 minutes, on a wire rack before slicing.

TIP: Prefer a soft crust? Place the cooled baked rolls in a resealable plastic bag overnight to soften.

PESTO DINNER ROLLS

I grew up in an Italian household where pesto was what you made every summer with the abundant basil growing in your garden. In this recipe, I mix pesto uniformly into the dough, making each bite a taste of the season.

YIELD: 4 (4-ounce) rolls **ACTIVE TIME:** 10 minutes
BAKE TIME: 35 minutes **TOTAL TIME:** 2 hours 35 minutes

TOOLS NEEDED

kitchen scale

stand mixer with paddle attachment or large bowl and dough whisk

parchment paper

3-ounce ice cream scoop or ⅓ cup measuring cup

offset spatula or spoon

plastic wrap

rimmed baking sheet

14.3-by-3.6-by-10.6-inch nonstick parchment paper cooking bag

heatproof clip (optional)

wire rack

INGREDIENTS

275g High-Protein Flour (page 32), plus more for dusting

3g (½ teaspoon) salt

128g lukewarm water (65°F)

2 large egg whites (60g), at room temperature, or 60g more lukewarm water (65°F)

2g (½ teaspoon) apple cider vinegar

45g store-bought or homemade pesto, stirred well (see Tip)

1. **COMBINE:** In a large bowl using a dough whisk or in the bowl of a stand mixer fitted with the paddle attachment, mix together the High-Protein Flour and salt on low speed. Add the water, egg whites, and vinegar; mix until combined. Increase the speed to medium and beat for 3 minutes to add air to the dough, incorporating the pesto little by little until well distributed.

2. **SHAPE:** Generously dust a piece of parchment paper with High-Protein Flour; using a wet 3-ounce ice cream scoop or ⅓ cup measuring cup, scoop the dough onto the parchment paper, spacing the rolls about 2 inches apart. Using a wet offset spatula or spoon, gently smooth out the surface of each roll.

3. **PROOF:** Cover loosely with plastic wrap and proof at room temperature until the dough is puffy, about 1½ hours.

4. **PREHEAT:** Place an inverted rimmed baking sheet on the middle rack of the oven and preheat to 400°F. Dust the top of the rolls with High-Protein Flour and slide the dough on the parchment paper into a parchment paper cooking bag; fold the bag opening several turns or use a heatproof clip to seal.

5. **BAKE:** Place the cooking bag on the preheated baking sheet and bake until the rolls are crusty and sound hollow when tapped on the bottom, about 35 minutes.

6. **COOL:** Carefully tear open the bag (hot steam will escape), remove the loaf, and let cool completely, about 20 minutes, on a wire rack before slicing.

TIP: In place of pesto, swap in romesco for a roasted red pepper flavor.

PUMPERNICKEL-STYLE BREAD

I grew up eating pumpernickel bread slathered with cream cheese and topped with capers, red onion, and lox. While it's typically made with glutenous rye flour, my take on pumpernickel swaps in caraway seeds to mimic that classic flavor profile.

YIELD: 1 (1-pound) loaf **ACTIVE TIME:** 10 minutes
BAKE TIME: 1 hour 20 minutes **TOTAL TIME:** 3 hours 30 minutes

TOOLS NEEDED

kitchen scale

stand mixer with paddle attachment or large bowl and dough whisk

parchment paper

offset spatula or spoon

plastic wrap

rimmed baking sheet

bread lame or sharp knife

14.3-by-3.6-by-10.6-inch nonstick parchment paper cooking bag

heatproof clip (optional)

wire rack

INGREDIENTS

275g High-Protein Flour (page 32), plus more for dusting

3g (½ teaspoon) salt

128g lukewarm water (65°F)

2 large egg whites (60g), at room temperature, or 60g more lukewarm water (65°F)

20g molasses

12g sunflower seed oil

2g (½ teaspoon) apple cider vinegar

4g (2 teaspoons) cocoa powder

2g (1 teaspoon) caraway seeds

1. **COMBINE:** In a large bowl using a dough whisk or in the bowl of a stand mixer fitted with the paddle attachment, mix together the High-Protein flour and salt on low speed. Add the water, egg whites, molasses, sunflower seed oil, vinegar, cocoa powder, and caraway seeds; mix until combined. Increase the speed to medium and beat for 3 minutes to add air to the dough.

2. **SHAPE:** Generously dust a piece of parchment paper with High-Protein Flour; place the dough onto the parchment paper. Using a wet offset spatula or spoon, shape the dough into a loaf and gently smooth out the surface.

3. **PROOF:** Lightly dust with High-Protein Flour again and cover loosely with plastic wrap; proof at room temperature until the dough is puffy, about 1½ hours.

4. **PREHEAT:** Place an inverted rimmed baking sheet on the middle rack of the oven and preheat to 400°F. Dust the dough with High-Protein Flour, then use a bread lame or sharp knife to score the surface of the bread dough in three places. Slide the dough on the parchment paper into a parchment paper cooking bag; fold the bag opening several turns or use a heatproof clip to seal.

5. **BAKE:** Place the cooking bag on the preheated baking sheet and bake until the loaf is crusty and sounds hollow when tapped on the bottom, about 1 hour 20 minutes.

6. **COOL:** Carefully tear open the bag (hot steam will escape), remove the loaf, and let cool completely, about 30 minutes, on a wire rack before slicing.

> **TIP:** Want even more rye-like flavor? Stir in about 2g (1 teaspoon) of ground caraway seeds into the dough along with the whole seeds.

FENNEL RAISIN SEMOLINA-STYLE BREAD

I've been addicted to the fennel raisin semolina loaf at Amy's Bread in Hell's Kitchen, NYC—its sweet golden raisins and anise-scented fennel seeds are to die for. To replace the semolina in the original recipe, I use medium-grind cornmeal.

YIELD: 1 (1-pound) loaf **ACTIVE TIME:** 10 minutes
BAKE TIME: 1 hour 20 minutes **TOTAL TIME:** 3 hours 30 minutes

TOOLS NEEDED

kitchen scale

small bowl

stand mixer with paddle attachment or large bowl and dough whisk

parchment paper

offset spatula or spoon

plastic wrap

rimmed baking sheet

bread lame or sharp knife

14.3-by-3.6-by-10.6-inch nonstick parchment paper cooking bag

heatproof clip (optional)

wire rack

INGREDIENTS

112g golden raisins

275g High-Protein Flour (page 32)

3g (½ teaspoon) salt

128g lukewarm water (65°F)

2 large egg whites (60g), at room temperature, or 60g more lukewarm water (65°F)

12g sunflower seed oil

2g (½ teaspoon) apple cider vinegar

4g (2 teaspoons) whole fennel seeds

2g (1 teaspoon) smashed or ground fennel seeds

Cornmeal, preferably medium grind, for dusting

1. **SOAK:** Place the raisins in a small bowl and cover with boiling water; soak for 5 minutes, then drain well.

2. **COMBINE:** In a large bowl using a dough whisk or in the bowl of a stand mixer fitted with the paddle attachment, mix together the High-Protein Flour and salt on low speed. Add the water, egg whites, sunflower seed oil, vinegar, drained raisins, and both types of fennel seed; mix until combined. Increase the speed to medium and beat for 3 minutes to add air to the dough.

3. **SHAPE:** Generously dust a piece of parchment paper with cornmeal; place the dough onto the parchment paper. Using a wet offset spatula or a spoon, shape the dough into a loaf shape and gently smooth out the surface.

4. **PROOF:** Cover loosely with plastic wrap and proof at room temperature until the dough is puffy, about 1½ hours.

5. **PREHEAT:** Place an inverted rimmed baking sheet on the middle rack of the oven and preheat to 400°F. Spray the dough with water, then dust generously with cornmeal and, using a bread lame or sharp knife, score the surface in three places. Slide the dough on the parchment paper into a parchment paper cooking bag; fold the bag opening several turns or use a heatproof clip to seal.

6. **BAKE:** Place the cooking bag on the preheated baking sheet and bake until the loaf is crusty and sounds hollow when tapped on the bottom, about 1 hour 20 minutes.

7. **COOL:** Carefully tear open the bag (hot steam will escape), remove the loaf, and let cool completely, about 30 minutes, on a wire rack before slicing.

TIP: Want a more traditional yellow bread crumb? Replace 76g (½ cup) of the High-Protein Flour with corn flour.

MUESLI FLATBREAD

I love eating these small flatbreads toasted, with salted butter and blackberry jam slathered on top. When I want extra protein, I spread the flatbread with crunchy almond or peanut butter.

YIELD: 6 (3-inch) flatbreads **ACTIVE TIME:** 10 minutes
COOK TIME: 10 minutes **TOTAL TIME:** 1 hour 50 minutes

TOOLS NEEDED

kitchen scale

stand mixer with paddle attachment
or large bowl and dough whisk

rolling pin

plastic wrap

cast-iron skillet

rimmed baking sheet

INGREDIENTS

275g High-Protein Flour (page 32),
plus more for dusting

10g millet flour

12g gluten-free old-fashioned
rolled oats

6g (1½ teaspoons) granulated sugar

4g (¾ teaspoon) salt

148g lukewarm water (65°F)

2 large egg whites (60g), at room
temperature, or 60g more lukewarm
water (65°F)

12g sunflower seed oil

2g (½ teaspoon) apple cider vinegar

20g raisins

15g chopped dried apples

1. **COMBINE:** In a large bowl using a dough whisk or in the bowl of a stand mixer fitted with the paddle attachment, mix together the High-Protein Flour, millet flour, oats, sugar, and salt on low speed. Add the water, egg whites, sunflower seed oil, vinegar, raisins, and dried apples; mix until combined. Increase the speed to medium and beat for 3 minutes to add air to the dough.

2. **SHAPE:** Place the dough on a clean surface that's been lightly dusted with High-Protein Flour. Divide the dough into six equal pieces and, using a rolling pin, loosely shape each into a circle about ¼ inch thick. (The diameter of the circle is not as important as the thickness of the dough, so don't worry about how big they are.)

3. **PROOF:** Cover loosely with plastic wrap and proof at room temperature until the dough is puffy, about 1½ hours.

4. **COOK:** Heat a dry cast-iron skillet over medium heat. Working in batches, place the dough into the hot pan and cook, turning once, until puffy, about 3 minutes. Transfer the flatbreads to a rimmed baking sheet to cool while you repeat with the remaining dough.

> **TIP:** Prefer to bake these in your oven? Just place an inverted rimmed baking sheet on the bottom rack and preheat your oven to 475°F. A few minutes before baking, lightly spray four dough rounds with water and set them on a sheet of parchment paper. Transfer with the paper onto the preheated baking sheet and bake until lightly golden, about 3 minutes. Repeat with the remaining dough.

OLIVE HERB BREAD TWISTS

This is my playful take on more traditional olive bread or rolls. The twists are easy and fun to eat. I prefer using mixed olives, but go ahead and use your favorite olive, including black Kalamata or green Castelvetrano olives. If you're using olives in brine with herbs, you can leave out the dried oregano.

YIELD: 12 (10-inch) twists **ACTIVE TIME:** 15 minutes
BAKE TIME: 25 minutes **TOTAL TIME:** 2 hours 30 minutes

TOOLS NEEDED

kitchen scale

stand mixer with paddle attachment or large bowl and dough whisk

9-by-13-inch baking sheet

nonstick cooking spray

parchment paper

rolling pin

pizza cutter or sharp knife

pastry brush

plastic wrap

rimmed baking sheet

wire rack

INGREDIENTS

550g High-Protein Flour (page 32), plus more for dusting

6g (1 teaspoon) salt

1g (1½ teaspoons) dried oregano

343g lukewarm water (65°F)

2 large egg whites (60g), at room temperature, or 60g more lukewarm water (65°F)

12g olive oil, plus more for brushing

2g (½ teaspoon) apple cider vinegar

90g pitted and drained coarsely chopped mixed olives

1. **COMBINE:** In a large bowl using a dough whisk or in the bowl of a stand mixer fitted with the paddle attachment, mix together the High-Protein Flour, salt, and oregano on low speed. Add the water, egg whites, olive oil, and vinegar; mix until combined. Increase the speed to medium and beat for 3 minutes to add air to the dough. Reduce the speed to low and add the olives; mix until just combined.

2. **SHAPE:** Generously grease a 9-by-13-inch baking sheet with nonstick cooking spray. On a clean work surface, lay out a piece of parchment paper and dust it lightly with High-Protein Flour. Scoop the dough onto the parchment paper. Using a floured rolling pin, roll the dough into a 9-by-13-inch rectangle about ½ inch thick. Using a pizza cutter or sharp knife, cut the dough into 12 equal strips, then gently lift and twist each piece and place them on the prepared baking sheet, about ⅛ inch apart.

3. **PROOF:** Use a pastry brush to lightly coat the twists with oil and cover loosely with plastic wrap; proof at room temperature until the dough is puffy, about 1½ hours.

4. **PREHEAT:** Place an inverted rimmed baking sheet on the middle rack of the oven and preheat to 400°F.

5. **BAKE:** Bake the bread twists until golden brown, 20 to 25 minutes.

6. **COOL:** Let cool completely, about 20 minutes, on a wire rack.

TIP: Worried about successfully twisting the bread dough? Just leave the dough in a breadstick-like log instead.

EVERYTHING BAGELS

Having lived in New York City for the past 27 years, I can't imagine a life without bagels. But that's not just nostalgia. Bagels are one of the most versatile breads you can bake—you can add flavors to the dough (think cinnamon raisin, pumpernickel, even jalapeño), and you can coat them with toppings such as sesame seeds, poppy seeds, onion, and garlic, like I do here.

YIELD: 6 (4.5-ounce) bagels **ACTIVE TIME:** 15 minutes
COOK TIME: 35 minutes **TOTAL TIME:** 2 hours 45 minutes

TOOLS NEEDED

kitchen scale

stand mixer with paddle attachment or large bowl and dough whisk

rimmed baking sheet

parchment paper

nonstick cooking spray

plastic wrap

large pot

slotted spoon

paper towels

pastry brush

wire rack

INGREDIENTS

550g High-Protein Flour (page 32)

15g salt, divided

413g lukewarm water (65°F)

28g brown rice syrup or corn syrup, divided

14g baking soda

1 large egg (57g) beaten with 15g water, for the egg wash

Everything bagel topping, for coating (see Tip)

1. **COMBINE:** In a large bowl with a dough whisk or in the bowl of a stand mixer fitted with the paddle attachment, mix together the High-Protein Flour and 9g (1½ teaspoons) of salt on low speed. Add the water and 7g (1 teaspoon) of brown rice syrup; mix until combined. Increase the speed to medium and beat for 3 minutes to add air to the dough.

2. **SHAPE:** Line a rimmed baking sheet with parchment paper and grease with nonstick cooking spray. Divide the dough into six equal pieces; cupping your hands, shape each into a ball. Poke a hole through the center of each and, using your thumb, rotate the dough, gradually stretching it, to form a 2-inch hole. Place the shaped dough on the prepared baking sheet and grease with cooking spray.

3. **PROOF:** Cover the dough with plastic wrap and proof until the dough is puffy, about 1½ hours.

4. **PREHEAT:** Preheat the oven to 475°F. In a large pot, bring 1,890g (8 cups) of water to a boil; reduce the heat to medium and stir in the baking soda, remaining 21g of brown rice syrup, and remaining 6g (1 teaspoon) of salt; bring to a simmer.

5. **BOIL:** Working with a few bagels at a time, lower the dough into the boiling water and cook, turning once, until they have risen to the surface, about 2 minutes. Remove them with a slotted spoon and drain on a paper towel. Line the baking sheet with a new piece of parchment paper, then lightly grease with cooking spray. Place the bagels, rounded side up, on the prepared baking sheet. Use a pastry brush to coat the bagels with the egg wash and sprinkle immediately with the everything bagel topping.

6. **BAKE:** Reduce the heat to 425°F and bake until browned, about 25 minutes.

7. **COOL:** Let cool completely, about 30 minutes, on a wire rack and serve warm or at room temperature.

TIP: Not into everything bagel topping? Just keep the bagels plain or top with poppy seeds, sesame seeds, or coarse salt.

JALAPEÑO CHEDDAR SOFT PRETZEL BITES

You know SuperPretzel, the classic glutenous soft pretzel you see in your supermarket's freezer section? These are the best of both SuperPretzel and the mall-favorite Auntie Anne's pretzels—chewy, puffy, salty, and sweet in one bite.

YIELD: About 24 (2-inch) bites **ACTIVE TIME:** 15 minutes
COOK TIME: 15 minutes **TOTAL TIME:** 1 hour

TOOLS NEEDED

kitchen scale

stand mixer with paddle attachment or large bowl and dough whisk

rimmed baking sheet

parchment paper

nonstick cooking spray

large pot

slotted spoon

paper towels

pastry brush

INGREDIENTS

275g High-Protein Flour (page 32), plus more for dusting

3g (½ teaspoon) salt

236g lukewarm water (65°F)

12g sunflower seed oil

13g packed brown sugar

15g pickled jalapeño pepper slices, drained and chopped

48g baking soda

1 large egg (57g) beaten with 15g water, for the egg wash

Shredded Cheddar cheese, for sprinkling

1. **COMBINE:** In a large bowl with a dough whisk or in the bowl of a stand mixer fitted with the paddle attachment, mix together the High-Protein Flour and salt on low speed. Add the water, sunflower seed oil, and brown sugar; mix until combined. Increase the speed to medium and beat for 3 minutes to add air to the dough, sprinkling in the jalapeño until incorporated.

2. **SHAPE:** Transfer the dough onto a clean surface lightly dusted with High-Protein Flour and cut it into golf ball–size pieces. Then roll them into ½-inch-thick ropes and cut into 2-inch pieces.

3. **PROOF:** Let stand at room temperature, uncovered, until the dough is puffy, about 30 minutes.

4. **BOIL:** Line a rimmed baking sheet with parchment paper, then lightly grease with nonstick cooking spray. In a large pot, bring 946g (4 cups) of water and the baking soda to a boil. Working in batches, drop about 12 dough pieces into the boiling water for 30 seconds. Remove with a slotted spoon and drain on a paper towel, then place on the prepared baking sheet. Repeat with the remaining dough, returning the water to a boil between batches if necessary.

5. **PREHEAT:** Preheat the oven to 475°F.

6. **BAKE:** Brush the dough pieces with the egg wash and sprinkle with Cheddar. Bake until browned and the cheese has melted, about 10 minutes. Serve warm or at room temperature.

> **TIP:** Prefer the classic pretzel shape? Form each dough rope into a U shape, cross the ends over each other twice to form the twist, then bring the ends to the bottom of the U and press the tips onto it.

PIZZA CRUST, PAGE 64

CHAPTER 4

SANDWICH BREADS AND PIZZA

Making gluten-free sandwich bread is a game changer. In this chapter, you'll find a basic loaf, a cinnamon-raisin version, and a honey, nuts, and oats bread. Then, there's the pizza. If you like garlic bread, you'll love my Garlic Butter Focaccia Bread (page 72), and the Parmesan Pull-Apart Pizza Breadsticks (page 76) are sure to be your new favorite dipper for winter soups.

SANDWICH LOAF BREAD

When you don't have to toast gluten-free bread before eating it, you know it's a seriously good loaf. The outside has just the right amount of bite while the inside crumb is soft and fluffy. Also, this bread is more of the standard sandwich size than most store-bought gluten-free versions.

YIELD: 1 (2-pound) loaf **ACTIVE TIME:** 15 minutes
BAKE TIME: 1 hour 10 minutes **TOTAL TIME:** 4 hours

TOOLS NEEDED

kitchen scale

stand mixer with paddle attachment or large bowl and dough whisk

5-by-9-inch cast-iron or metal loaf pan

nonstick cooking spray

offset spatula or spoon

plastic wrap

rimmed baking sheet

food thermometer

wire rack

INGREDIENTS

550g High-Protein Flour (page 32)

472g lukewarm water (65°F)

4 large egg whites (120g), at room temperature, lightly beaten, or 120g more lukewarm water (65°F)

24g sunflower seed oil

1. **COMBINE:** In a large bowl with a dough whisk or in the bowl of a stand mixer fitted with the paddle attachment, mix together the High-Protein Flour, water, egg whites, and sunflower seed oil on low speed until combined. Increase the speed to medium and beat for 3 minutes to add air to the dough.

2. **SHAPE:** Grease a loaf pan with nonstick cooking spray. Transfer the dough into the loaf pan and, using a wet offset spatula or spoon, gently smooth out the surface.

3. **PROOF:** Cover loosely with plastic wrap and proof at room temperature until the dough domes over the edge of the pan, about 1½ hours.

4. **PREHEAT:** Place an inverted rimmed baking sheet on the middle rack of the oven and preheat to 425°F.

5. **BAKE:** Bake for 15 minutes, then reduce the heat to 350°F and bake for 30 minutes more. Remove the loaf from the pan, set on the preheated baking sheet, and bake until golden and the internal temperature measures 208°F, 20 to 25 minutes more.

6. **COOL:** Let cool completely, about 1 hour, on a wire rack.

TIP: If you have an instant-read thermometer, you can measure the interior of the bread to see if it's cooked through. Just be sure to place the thermometer in the center of the loaf.

PIZZA CRUST

My mission in developing a pizza crust was to make a low-maintenance dough that could roll out easily, puff up nicely, and taste delicious. Mission accomplished. I also wanted to be able to freeze a prebaked crust so it could be ready at a moment's notice. You can freeze these baked pizza crusts for up to 1 month; just bring to room temperature before topping and baking.

YIELD: 2 (8½-inch) pizzas **ACTIVE TIME:** 10 minutes
BAKE TIME: 16 minutes **TOTAL TIME:** 1 hour

TOOLS NEEDED

kitchen scale

large bowl

dough whisk

wooden spoon

parchment paper

rolling pin (optional)

plastic wrap

rimmed baking sheet

pastry brush

wire rack

cutting board

pizza cutter or serrated knife

INGREDIENTS

320g All-Purpose Flour (page 31), plus more for dusting

7g (one ¼-ounce package) instant yeast

4g (1 teaspoon) granulated sugar

6g (1 teaspoon) salt

177g lukewarm water (65°F)

2 large egg whites (60g), at room temperature, lightly beaten, or 60g lukewarm water (65°F)

24g olive oil, plus more for brushing

112g (½ cup) store-bought or homemade pizza sauce, for topping, divided

Various toppings, such as thinly sliced bell peppers, onions, mushrooms, pepperoni, cooked sausage slices, mozzarella, Parmesan cheese, olives

1. **COMBINE:** In a large bowl, use a dough whisk to combine the All-Purpose Flour, yeast, sugar, and salt. Add the water, egg whites, and olive oil. Using a wooden spoon, beat until the dough pulls away from the sides of the bowl.

2. **SHAPE:** Divide the dough into two equal pieces. Dust a piece of parchment paper lightly with All-Purpose Flour and transfer one of the dough portions onto it. Dust it with more All-Purpose Flour and, using your fingertips or a rolling pin, press the dough out to a circle about 8½ inches across and ¼ inch thick. Repeat with the second portion of dough.

3. **PROOF:** Cover loosely with plastic wrap and proof at room temperature for about 30 minutes.

4. **PREHEAT:** Place an inverted rimmed baking sheet on the bottom rack of the oven and preheat to 450°F.

5. **BAKE:** One portion of dough at a time, slide the dough with its parchment paper onto the preheated baking sheet and bake until puffy, golden, and crisp on the bottom, about 8 minutes. Repeat with the remaining dough.

6. **MAKE THE PIZZA:** Working with one pizza crust at a time, brush with olive oil. Spoon on about 56g (¼ cup) of pizza sauce, leaving a ½-inch border, then cover with your favorite toppings. Bake until the crust is golden, about 8 minutes. Repeat with the remaining crust and toppings.

7. **COOL:** Let cool slightly on a wire rack, about 5 minutes, then transfer each pizza to a cutting board and, using a pizza cutter or serrated knife, cut each round into four pieces.

TIP: For an even crispier crust, I recommend using a baking stone, which you can order online for about $30.

SESAME SANDWICH BREAD SQUARES

Once I figured out how to make gluten-free pizza dough, these ciabatta-like squares weren't far behind. I call them bread squares because I roll out the dough about ¾ inch thick and cut it into four squares—it's that easy. When you're ready to make a sandwich, just slice it in half crosswise and stuff with your favorite fillings.

YIELD: 4 (4-ounce) sandwich squares **ACTIVE TIME:** 10 minutes
BAKE TIME: 10 minutes **TOTAL TIME:** 1 hour 10 minutes

TOOLS NEEDED

kitchen scale

large bowl

dough whisk

wooden spoon

parchment paper

rolling pin (optional)

plastic wrap

rimmed baking sheet

wire rack

INGREDIENTS

320g All-Purpose Flour (page 31), plus more for dusting

7g (one ¼-ounce package) instant yeast

4g (1 teaspoon) granulated sugar

6g (1 teaspoon) salt

177g lukewarm water (65°F)

2 large egg whites (60g), at room temperature, lightly beaten, or 60g lukewarm water (65°F)

24g olive oil, plus more for brushing

Sesame seeds, for sprinkling

1. **COMBINE:** In a large bowl, use a dough whisk to combine the All-Purpose Flour, yeast, sugar, and salt. Add the water, egg whites, and olive oil. Using a wooden spoon, beat until the dough pulls away from the sides of the bowl, about 3 minutes.

2. **SHAPE:** Lightly dust a piece of parchment paper with All-Purpose Flour. Turn the dough onto the parchment and lightly dust the top with more All-Purpose Flour. Using your fingertips or a rolling pin, press the dough out into an 8-inch square about ¾ inch thick.

3. **PROOF:** Cover loosely with plastic wrap and proof at room temperature until the dough is puffy, about 30 minutes.

4. **PREHEAT:** Place an inverted rimmed baking sheet on the middle rack of the oven and preheat to 450°F. Cut the dough into four equal pieces. Spray lightly with water and sprinkle with sesame seeds.

5. **BAKE:** Slide the dough pieces with their parchment paper onto the preheated baking sheet and bake until puffy and crisp on the bottom, about 10 minutes.

6. **COOL:** Let cool completely, about 20 minutes, on a wire rack.

> **TIP:** If you prefer plain sandwich squares, dust with All-Purpose Flour (page 31) just before baking instead.

CINNAMON-RAISIN SANDWICH BREAD

This sandwich bread is perfect on its own, toasted with butter, or used to make French toast. Some of my favorite sandwich fillings to go with this bread include curry chicken salad, ham and Cheddar, or even Thanksgiving leftovers.

YIELD: 1 (2-pound) loaf **ACTIVE TIME:** 15 minutes
BAKE TIME: 1 hour 10 minutes **TOTAL TIME:** 4 hours

TOOLS NEEDED

kitchen scale

stand mixer with paddle attachment or large bowl and dough whisk

5-by-9-inch cast-iron or metal loaf pan

nonstick cooking spray

offset spatula or spoon

plastic wrap

rimmed baking sheet

food thermometer

small bowl

pastry brush

wire rack

INGREDIENTS

550g High-Protein Flour (page 32)

472g lukewarm water (65°F)

4 large egg whites (120g), at room temperature, lightly beaten, or 120g more lukewarm water (65°F)

24g sunflower seed oil

50g packed brown sugar

13g ground cinnamon, divided

225g raisins

50g granulated sugar

Melted unsalted butter, for brushing

1. **COMBINE:** In a large bowl with a dough whisk or in the bowl of a stand mixer fitted with the paddle attachment, mix together the High-Protein Flour, water, egg whites, sunflower seed oil, brown sugar, 8g (1 tablespoon) of cinnamon, and raisins on low speed until combined. Increase the speed to medium and beat for 3 minutes to add air to the dough.

2. **SHAPE:** Grease a loaf pan with nonstick cooking spray. Transfer the dough into the loaf pan and, using a wet offset spatula or spoon, gently smooth out the surface.

3. **PROOF:** Cover loosely with plastic wrap and proof at room temperature until the dough domes over the edge of the pan, about 1½ hours.

4. **PREHEAT:** Place an inverted rimmed baking sheet on the middle rack of the oven and preheat to 425°F.

5. **BAKE:** Bake for 15 minutes, then reduce the heat to 350°F and bake for 30 minutes more. Remove the loaf from the pan, set on the preheated baking sheet, and bake until golden and the internal temperature measures 208°F, 20 to 25 minutes more.

6. **COOL:** In a small bowl, stir together the granulated sugar and remaining 5g (2 teaspoons) of cinnamon. Remove the loaf from the oven and brush with butter, then quickly coat it in the cinnamon sugar. Let cool completely, about 1 hour, on a wire rack.

TIP: For a glossy finish, brush the loaf hot out of the oven with simple syrup. To make it, in a small saucepan, bring 67g (⅓ cup) granulated sugar and 120g (½ cup) water to a boil. Reduce the heat to medium and cook until the sugar dissolves, about 2 minutes.

HONEY, NUTS, AND OATS SANDWICH BREAD

I grew up on Honey Bunches of Oats and Honey Nut Cheerios—both of which inspired the nostalgic flavor combinations in this sandwich bread.

YIELD: 1 (2-pound) loaf **ACTIVE TIME:** 15 minutes
BAKE TIME: 1 hour 10 minutes **TOTAL TIME:** 4 hours

TOOLS NEEDED

kitchen scale

stand mixer with paddle attachment or large bowl and dough whisk

5-by-9-inch cast-iron or metal loaf pan

nonstick cooking spray

offset spatula or spoon

plastic wrap

rimmed baking sheet

food thermometer

pastry brush

wire rack

INGREDIENTS

550g High-Protein Flour (page 32)

413g lukewarm water (65°F)

4 large egg whites (120g), at room temperature, lightly beaten, or 120g more lukewarm water (65°F)

42g honey, plus more for brushing

24g sunflower seed oil

65g chopped pecans

Gluten-free oat bran, for coating (see Tip)

Gluten-free old-fashioned rolled oats, for sprinkling

1. **COMBINE:** In a large bowl with a dough whisk or in the bowl of a stand mixer fitted with the paddle attachment, mix together the High-Protein Flour, water, egg whites, honey, sunflower seed oil, and pecans on low speed until combined. Increase the speed to medium and beat for 3 minutes to add air to the dough.

2. **SHAPE:** Grease a loaf pan with nonstick cooking spray and coat the sides with oat bran. Transfer the dough into the loaf pan and, using a wet offset spatula or spoon, gently smooth out the surface.

3. **PROOF:** Cover loosely with plastic wrap and proof at room temperature until the dough domes over the edge of the pan, about 1½ hours.

4. **PREHEAT:** Place an inverted rimmed baking sheet on the middle rack of the oven and preheat to 425°F.

5. **BAKE:** Bake for 15 minutes, then reduce the heat to 350°F and bake for 30 minutes more. Remove the loaf from the pan, set on the preheated baking sheet, and bake until golden and the internal temperature measures 208°F, 20 to 25 minutes more. Remove from the oven, brush generously with honey, and sprinkle with oat bran and rolled oats.

6. **COOL:** Let cool completely, about 1 hour, on a wire rack.

TIP: If you can't find oat bran, swap in rice bran or just leave it out.

GARLIC BUTTER FOCACCIA BREAD

For this recipe, I merged two of my favorites—garlic bread and focaccia. The truth is, this focaccia bread is good enough to eat simply sprinkled with coarse salt.

YIELD: 1 (17.5-by-13.5-inch) focaccia **ACTIVE TIME:** 20 minutes
BAKE TIME: 25 minutes **TOTAL TIME:** 2 hours 20 minutes

TOOLS NEEDED

kitchen scale

stand mixer with paddle attachment or large bowl and dough whisk

two rimmed baking sheets

plastic wrap

small saucepan with lid

pastry brush

wire rack

cutting board

pizza cutter or serrated knife

INGREDIENTS

For the dough

550g High-Protein Flour (page 32)

413g lukewarm water (65°F)

4 large egg whites (120g), at room temperature, lightly beaten, or 120g more lukewarm water (65°F)

24g olive oil, plus more for greasing

For the garlic butter

57g (¼ cup) unsalted butter, melted

2g (¾ teaspoon) garlic powder

3g (½ teaspoon) salt

1. **COMBINE:** In a large bowl with a dough whisk or in the bowl of a stand mixer fitted with the paddle attachment, mix together the High-Protein Flour, water, egg whites, and olive oil on low speed until combined. Increase the speed to medium and beat for 3 minutes to add air to the dough.

2. **SHAPE:** Generously grease a rimmed baking sheet with olive oil. Transfer the dough to the prepared baking sheet. Lightly grease your hands and use your fingertips to gently dimple the dough, stretching it to the edges of the baking sheet.

3. **PROOF:** Cover loosely with plastic wrap and proof at room temperature until the dough is puffy, about 1½ hours.

4. **PREHEAT:** Place an inverted rimmed baking sheet on the middle rack of the oven and preheat to 400°F.

5. **BAKE:** Place the baking sheet with the dough on the preheated baking sheet and bake until golden, 20 to 25 minutes.

6. **MAKE THE GARLIC BUTTER:** Meanwhile, in a small saucepan over medium-low heat, combine the butter, garlic powder, and salt, stirring occasionally, until melted. Reduce the heat to low, cover, and keep warm.

7. **COOL:** Remove the focaccia from the oven and use a pastry brush to coat it thoroughly with the garlic butter. Let cool slightly on a wire rack, about 5 minutes, then transfer to a cutting board and use a pizza cutter or serrated knife to slice into pieces.

TIP: Want to spice things up? Stir 1g (½ teaspoon) red pepper flakes into the garlic butter.

CHICAGO DEEP-DISH PEPPERONI PAN PIZZA

Whether you think of Pizza Hut, Giordano's, or Lou Malnati's, you know what deep-dish pizza means—a thick, chewy crust that's perfect for loading on plenty of ingredients.

YIELD: 2 (9-inch) pizzas **ACTIVE TIME:** 20 minutes
BAKE TIME: 25 minutes **TOTAL TIME:** 2 hours 20 minutes

TOOLS NEEDED

kitchen scale

stand mixer with paddle attachment or large bowl and dough whisk

two 9-inch round cake pans

parchment paper

rolling pin

plastic wrap

rimmed baking sheet

wire rack

cutting board

pizza cutter or serrated knife

INGREDIENTS

550g High-Protein Flour (page 32), plus more for dusting

413g lukewarm water (65°F)

4 large egg whites (120g), at room temperature, lightly beaten, or 120g more lukewarm water (65°F)

24g olive oil, plus more for greasing

112g (½ cup) store-bought or home-made pizza sauce

169g (1½ cups) shredded mozzarella

24 small slices gluten-free pepperoni (see Tip)

1. **COMBINE:** In a large bowl with a dough whisk or in the bowl of a stand mixer fitted with the paddle attachment, mix together the High-Protein Flour, water, egg whites, and olive oil on low speed until combined. Increase the speed to medium and beat for 3 minutes to add air to the dough.

2. **SHAPE:** Generously grease two 9-inch round cake pans with olive oil. Divide the dough into two equal pieces. Dust a piece of parchment paper lightly with High-Protein Flour and transfer one of the dough portions onto it. Using a floured rolling pin, roll the dough into a 9-inch circle and place in one of the prepared pans. Repeat with the second portion of dough.

3. **PROOF:** Cover the pans loosely with plastic wrap and proof at room temperature until the dough is puffy, about 1½ hours.

4. **PREHEAT:** Place an inverted rimmed baking sheet on the middle rack of the oven and preheat to 400°F.

5. **BAKE:** Top each pizza round equally with sauce, mozzarella, and pepperoni. Bake until golden and bubbling, 20 to 25 minutes.

6. **COOL:** Let cool slightly on a wire rack, about 5 minutes, then transfer to a cutting board and use a pizza cutter or serrated knife to cut each round into four pieces.

TIP: Vegetarian? Swap in your favorite pizza toppings for the pepperoni.

PARMESAN PULL-APART PIZZA BREADSTICKS

Remember Pizza Hut or Little Caesars? These copycat breadsticks will deliver those chewy-crisp memories in no time.

YIELD: 12 (10-inch) breadsticks **ACTIVE TIME:** 15 minutes
BAKE TIME: 25 minutes **TOTAL TIME:** 2 hours 10 minutes

TOOLS NEEDED

kitchen scale

stand mixer with paddle attachment or large bowl and dough whisk

small bowl

two rimmed baking sheets

parchment paper

rolling pin

pizza cutter or sharp knife

pastry brush

plastic wrap

INGREDIENTS

550g High-Protein Flour (page 32), plus more for dusting

343g lukewarm water (65°F)

2 large egg whites (60g), at room temperature, lightly beaten, or 60g more lukewarm water (65°F)

60g olive oil, plus more for greasing and brushing

12g salt, divided

9g (1 tablespoon) garlic powder, divided

7g (2 tablespoons) Italian seasoning blend

Grated Parmesan cheese, for sprinkling (see Tip)

Homemade or store-bought marinara sauce, warmed, for dipping

1. **COMBINE:** In a large bowl with a dough whisk or in the bowl of a stand mixer fitted with the paddle attachment, mix together the High-Protein Flour, water, egg whites, olive oil, 6g (1 teaspoon) of salt, and 3g (1 teaspoon) of garlic powder on low speed until combined. Increase the speed to medium and beat for 3 minutes to add air to the dough. In a small bowl, stir together the Italian seasoning blend, remaining 6g (2 teaspoons) of garlic powder, and remaining 6g (1 teaspoon) of salt to make a pizza seasoning. Set aside.

2. **SHAPE:** Generously grease a rimmed baking sheet with olive oil. Dust a piece of parchment paper lightly with High-Protein Flour and transfer the dough onto it. Using a floured rolling pin, roll out the dough into a 9-by-13-inch rectangle about ½ inch thick. Using a pizza cutter or sharp knife, cut into 12 equal strips and place on the prepared baking sheet about ⅛ inch apart. Use a pastry brush to coat the dough with olive oil and sprinkle generously with Parmesan cheese and the pizza seasoning.

3. **PROOF:** Cover loosely with plastic wrap and proof at room temperature until the dough is puffy, about 1½ hours.

4. **PREHEAT:** Place an inverted rimmed baking sheet on the middle rack and preheat the oven to 400°F.

5. **BAKE:** Place the baking sheet with the dough on the preheated baking sheet and bake until golden brown, about 25 minutes. Serve hot with the marinara dipping sauce.

TIP: Dairy-free? Swap in vegan Parmesan-style cheese or leave it out.

MUFFALETTA-STYLE PIZZA

Filled with Italian charcuterie and Creole olive salad, the muffaletta sandwich was invented in 1906 by Lupo Salvatore. This recipe is my take on the classic—pizza-style.

YIELD: 2 (8½-inch) pizzas **ACTIVE TIME:** 10 minutes
BAKE TIME: 30 minutes **TOTAL TIME:** 1 hour 15 minutes

TOOLS NEEDED

kitchen scale

large bowl

dough whisk

wooden spoon

parchment paper

rolling pin (optional)

plastic wrap

rimmed baking sheet

medium bowl

pastry brush

wire rack

cutting board

pizza cutter or serrated knife

INGREDIENTS

1 Pizza Crust recipe (dough only, page 64)

Sesame seeds, for sprinkling

60g (¼ cup) pimiento-stuffed olives, chopped

80g (¼ cup) jarred roasted red peppers, drained and chopped

65g (¼ cup) giardiniera, drained well and chopped (see Tip)

2½g (1 teaspoon) capers, rinsed and drained well

1 shallot, finely chopped (about 25g)

12g (1 tablespoon) olive oil, plus more for brushing

2½g (½ teaspoon) red wine vinegar

Salt

34g (¼ cup) roughly chopped ham

34g (¼ cup) roughly chopped salami

34g (¼ cup) roughly chopped mortadella (optional)

112g (1 cup) shredded provolone

1. **MAKE THE DOUGH:** Follow step 1 on page 65 to create the pizza dough, using the measurements on that page.

2. **SHAPE:** Divide the dough into two equal pieces. Lightly dust a piece of parchment paper with High-Protein Flour and transfer one of the dough portions onto it. Sprinkle generously with sesame seeds and, using your fingertips or a rolling pin, press the dough into a circle about 8½ inches across and ¼ inch thick.

3. **PROOF:** Cover loosely with plastic wrap and proof at room temperature until the dough is puffy, about 30 minutes.

4. **PREHEAT:** Place an inverted rimmed baking sheet on the bottom rack of the oven and preheat to 450°F.

5. **BAKE:** Working one pizza at a time, slide the dough with its parchment paper onto the preheated baking sheet and bake until puffy, golden, and crisp on the bottom, about 8 minutes. Repeat with the remaining dough.

6. **MAKE THE SAUCE:** Meanwhile, in a medium bowl, combine the olives, red peppers, giardiniera, capers, shallots, olive oil, and vinegar. Season with salt to taste.

7. **BAKE THE MUFFALETTA PIZZAS:** Brush each pizza crust with olive oil and spread with half of the sauce, leaving a ½-inch border. Top each with half of the ham, salami, mortadella (if using), and provolone. Place the pizzas directly on the preheated baking sheet and bake until the cheese is melted, 6 to 8 minutes.

8. **COOL:** Cool slightly, about 5 minutes, on a wire rack, then transfer each pizza to a cutting board and, using a pizza cutter or serrated knife, cut each round into four pieces.

TIP: Giardiniera, which literally means "woman gardener" in Italian, is a classic relish of pickled vegetables—carrots, cauliflower, red peppers, and celery. It's packed in vinegar, herbs, and spices as a way of preserving the summer harvest.

TRIPLE BERRY CREAM CHEESE DANISHES, PAGE 98

CHAPTER 5

ENRICHED BREADS

You may have never thought to attempt an enriched bread . . . until now. These rich, indulgent breads are the same as—if not better than—their glutenous counterparts. Get ready for versatile brioche bread dough that can be a loaf one day and a danish the next.

BRIOCHE LOAF BREAD

There's nothing quite as good as enjoying brioche slathered with salted butter and jam. I recommend proofing the dough overnight, which yields a lighter, more open crumb.

YIELD: 2 (½-pound) loaves **ACTIVE TIME:** 25 minutes **BAKE TIME:** 35 minutes
TOTAL TIME: 8 hours 40 minutes to 12 hours 40 minutes
(depending on your proofing method)

TOOLS NEEDED

kitchen scale

stand mixer with paddle attachment or large bowl and dough whisk

plastic wrap

two small bowls

two mini (5½-by-3-by-2¼-inch) loaf pans or one (5-by-9-inch) loaf pan

nonstick cooking spray

offset spatula or spoon

rimmed baking sheet

pastry brush

14.3-by-3.6-by-10.6-inch nonstick parchment paper cooking bag

heatproof clip (optional)

wire rack

INGREDIENTS

224g All-Purpose Flour (page 31), divided

4 large eggs (228g), at room temperature, divided

50g whole milk, heated to 100°F

3g (1 teaspoon) instant yeast

38g granulated sugar

3g (½ teaspoon) salt, plus 1 pinch

85g unsalted butter, at room temperature

1. **START THE DOUGH:** In a large bowl with a dough whisk or in the bowl of a stand mixer fitted with a paddle attachment, mix together 120g of All-Purpose Flour, 1 egg (57g), the milk, and yeast on low speed. Increase

the speed to medium and beat for 3 minutes to add air to the dough. Cover the dough loosely with plastic wrap and proof at room temperature until the dough is puffy, about 40 minutes.

2. **FINISH THE DOUGH:** In a small bowl, lightly beat 2 more eggs (114g). To the proofed dough, add 60g of All-Purpose Flour, the sugar, 3g (½ teaspoon) of salt, and the beaten eggs. Mix on low speed to combine, about 1 minute. With the motor running, gradually add the remaining 44g of All-Purpose Flour until combined, then increase the speed to medium and beat for 15 minutes to add air to the dough, scraping down the bowl as needed. Reduce the speed to medium-low and gradually add the butter. Increase the speed to medium and beat for 5 minutes more to completely incorporate, scraping down the bowl as needed.

3. **SHAPE:** Grease two mini loaf pans with nonstick cooking spray and evenly divide the dough between the two pans (or pour it all into one greased standard loaf pan). Using a wet offset spatula or spoon, gently smooth out the surface of each dough.

4. **PROOF:** Cover loosely with plastic wrap and proof at room temperature until the dough is puffy, about 1½ hours. Grease the dough with cooking spray and cover tightly with plastic wrap; refrigerate for 4 to 6 hours or, for a lighter texture, overnight.

5. **PREHEAT:** Remove the dough from the refrigerator and return to room temperature, about 1 hour. Meanwhile, place an inverted rimmed baking sheet on the middle rack of the oven and preheat to 350°F.

6. **MAKE THE EGG WASH:** In a small bowl, whisk together the remaining egg (57g) and pinch of salt; use a pastry brush to gently coat the dough with egg wash and place both loaf pans into a parchment paper cooking bag, folding the bag opening several turns or using a heatproof clip to seal.

7. **BAKE:** Place the cooking bag on the preheated baking sheet and bake for 25 minutes. Carefully tear open the bag (hot steam will escape) and continue to bake until golden, about 10 minutes more.

8. **COOL:** Let cool completely, about 30 minutes, on a wire rack before slicing.

BLUEBERRY BRIOCHE BUNS WITH STREUSEL TOPPING

Each summer, I love to go blueberry picking at my local berry farm upstate, which inspired me to make this recipe. The easy-to-make streusel topping takes these buns to the next level of deliciousness.

YIELD: 6 (6-ounce) buns **ACTIVE TIME:** 25 minutes **BAKE TIME:** 30 minutes
TOTAL TIME: 8 hours 25 minutes to 12 hours 25 minutes
(depending on your proofing method)

TOOLS NEEDED

kitchen scale

stand mixer with paddle attachment or large bowl and dough whisk

plastic wrap

two small bowls

two rimmed baking sheets

parchment paper

nonstick cooking spray

six 3-inch English muffin rings or mason jar lid rings

offset spatula or spoon

medium bowls

whisk

fork (optional)

pastry brush

wire rack

INGREDIENTS

For the dough

224g All-Purpose Flour (page 31), divided

50g whole milk, heated to 100°F

3g (1 teaspoon) instant yeast

4 large eggs (228g), at room temperature, divided

38g granulated sugar

3g (½ teaspoon) salt, plus 1 pinch

2g (¾ teaspoon) ground cinnamon

85g unsalted butter, at room temperature

83g blueberries, tossed in All-Purpose Flour (page 31) to coat

For the streusel topping

32g (¼ cup) All-Purpose Flour (page 31)

55g (¼ cup) packed brown sugar

50g (¼ cup) granulated sugar

1g (½ teaspoon) ground cinnamon

56g (4 tablespoons) unsalted butter, at room temperature

Confectioners' sugar, for dusting

1. **START THE DOUGH:** In a large bowl with a dough whisk or in the bowl of a stand mixer fitted with a paddle attachment, mix together 120g of All-Purpose Flour, the milk, yeast, and 1 egg (57g) on low speed. Increase the speed to medium and beat for 3 minutes to add air to the dough. Cover the dough loosely with plastic wrap and proof at room temperature until the dough is puffy, about 40 minutes.

2. **FINISH THE DOUGH:** In a small bowl, lightly beat 2 more eggs (114g). To the proofed dough, add 60g of All-Purpose Flour, the sugar, 3g (½ teaspoon) of salt, the cinnamon, and beaten eggs. Mix on low speed to combine, about 1 minute. With the motor running, gradually add the remaining 44g of All-Purpose Flour until combined, then increase the speed to medium and beat for 15 minutes to add air to the dough, scraping down the bowl as needed. Reduce the speed to medium-low and gradually add the butter. Increase the speed to medium and beat for 5 minutes more to completely incorporate, scraping down the bowl as needed. Reduce the speed to low and add the blueberries until just combined.

3. **SHAPE:** Line a rimmed baking sheet with parchment paper and grease with nonstick cooking spray. Grease six English muffin rings (or use the rings from 3-inch mason jar lids) with cooking spray and place them on the baking sheet. Divide the dough into six equal pieces and place into the rings. Using an offset spatula or wet spoon, gently smooth out the surface of each dough to fit the width of the ring.

4. **PROOF:** Cover loosely with plastic wrap and proof at room temperature until the dough is puffy, about 1½ hours. Grease the dough with cooking spray and cover tightly with plastic wrap; refrigerate for 4 to 6 hours or, for a lighter texture, overnight.

CONTINUED ▷

5. **PREHEAT:** Remove the dough from the refrigerator and return to room temperature, about 1 hour. Meanwhile, place an inverted rimmed baking sheet on the middle rack of the oven and preheat to 350°F.

6. **MAKE THE STREUSEL TOPPING:** In a medium bowl, whisk together the All-Purpose Flour, brown sugar, granulated sugar, and cinnamon. Add the butter and, using your fingers or a fork, blend together until coarse crumbs form.

7. **MAKE THE EGG WASH:** In a small bowl, whisk together the remaining egg (57g) and pinch of salt; use a pastry brush to gently coat the dough with egg wash and top with the streusel.

8. **BAKE:** Transfer the baking sheet onto the preheated baking sheet and bake until golden, about 30 minutes.

9. **COOL:** Let cool completely, about 20 minutes, on a wire rack. To serve, dust with confectioners' sugar.

TIP: If you don't have ring molds, you can bake these buns in a six-cup jumbo muffin pan.

ICED SNICKERDOODLE ROLLS

Cinnamon rolls are one of my most requested recipes, which is no surprise given their comfort-level status and hard-to-achieve texture as gluten-free treats. The flavors in this recipe are based on a favorite cookie of mine—the snickerdoodle, a generously spiced sugar-coated butter cookie.

YIELD: 16 (2-ounce) rolls **ACTIVE TIME:** 40 minutes **BAKE TIME:** 30 minutes
TOTAL TIME: 2 hours 30 minutes to 10 hours 30 minutes
(depending on your proofing method)

TOOLS NEEDED

kitchen scale

stand mixer with paddle attachment
or large bowl and dough whisk

two medium bowls

two 9-inch metal pie pans

nonstick cooking spray

rolling pin

serrated knife

plastic wrap

rimmed baking sheet

whisk

wire rack

INGREDIENTS

For the dough

550g High-Protein Flour (page 32),
plus more for dusting

413g whole milk, heated to 100°F

2 large eggs (114 g), at
room temperature

57g unsalted butter, at room
temperature (see Tip)

8g (2 teaspoons) pure vanilla extract

50g granulated sugar

6g (1 teaspoon) salt

1g (½ teaspoon) ground cardamom

CONTINUED ▷

For the filling

200g (1 cup) packed brown sugar

8g (1 tablespoon) ground cinnamon

1g (⅛ teaspoon) salt

28g (2 tablespoons) unsalted butter, melted (see Tip)

For the icing

375g (3 cups) confectioners' sugar

123g (½ cup) whole milk, at room temperature (see Tip)

85g (6 tablespoons) unsalted butter, melted (see Tip)

2g (¾ teaspoon) ground cinnamon

1g (¼ teaspoon) salt

1. **COMBINE THE DOUGH:** In a large bowl with a dough whisk or in the bowl of a stand mixer fitted with a paddle attachment, mix together the High-Protein Flour, milk, eggs, butter, vanilla, granulated sugar, salt, and cardamom, on low speed. Increase the speed to medium and beat for 3 minutes to add air to the dough.

2. **MAKE THE FILLING:** In a medium bowl, combine the brown sugar, cinnamon, salt, and melted butter.

3. **SHAPE:** Grease two 9-inch metal pie pans with nonstick cooking spray. Dust a clean work surface with High-Protein Flour and transfer the dough onto it. Using a rolling pin, roll the dough out to form a rectangle about 18 inches by 8 inches and ¼ inch thick. Scatter the filling over the dough, leaving about a ½-inch border. Beginning with the long edge nearest you, roll the dough into a cylinder and place it seam-side down. Using a serrated knife, cut the log crosswise into 16 rolls.

4. **PROOF:** Place half the rolls, cut-side down, in a circular pattern in each prepared pan and cover with plastic wrap. Proof at room temperature until puffy, about 1 hour, or refrigerate overnight (let warm to room temperature before baking, about 1 hour).

5. **PREHEAT:** About 20 minutes before baking, place an inverted rimmed baking sheet on the middle rack of the oven and preheat to 375°F.

6. **BAKE:** Bake the rolls until puffed and golden, 25 to 30 minutes.

7. **MAKE THE ICING:** While the rolls are baking, in a medium bowl, whisk together the confectioners' sugar, milk, butter, cinnamon, and salt until smooth.

8. **COOL:** Let the rolls cool on a wire rack for at least 10 minutes before spreading with icing and serving warm.

TIP: Dairy-free? Swap in nonhydrogenated shortening for the unsalted butter. In place of the milk, use your favorite dairy-free milk.

SESAME FLATBREAD WITH RED ONION DIP

This flatbread was inspired by naan, a yeasted flatbread that incorporates yogurt into the dough. The yogurt, which is fermented, gives the bread acidity, making it tender and fluffy.

MAKES: 6 (10-inch) flatbreads **ACTIVE TIME:** 40 minutes
COOK TIME: 38 minutes **TOTAL TIME:** 1 hour 15 minutes

TOOLS NEEDED

kitchen scale

cast-iron skillet

blender

large bowl

whisk

rolling pin

rimmed baking sheet

INGREDIENTS

For the dip

24g (2 tablespoons) olive oil

2 large red onions, halved crosswise, then cut into thin half-moons (about 200g or 4 cups)

3g (½ teaspoon) salt, plus more as needed

½g (¼ teaspoon) freshly ground black pepper, plus more as needed

1 garlic clove, minced (about 5g)

125g (½ cup) sour cream

45g (3 tablespoons) water

6g (1 teaspoon) gluten-free tamari

For the flatbread

550g High-Protein Flour (page 32), plus more for dusting

9g (1½ teaspoons) salt

295g to 355g lukewarm water (65°F)

70g plain yogurt, at room temperature

36g olive oil

20g sesame seeds, for sprinkling

1. **MAKE THE DIP:** Set a large cast-iron skillet over medium-high heat. Add the olive oil, onions, salt, and pepper. Cook, stirring occasionally, until the onions are softened, about 10 minutes. Stir in the garlic and cook until the onions are lightly browned, about 10 minutes more; let cool for about 15 minutes. Transfer ½ cup of the cooked onions to a blender and add the sour cream, the water, and tamari; puree until smooth and transfer to a bowl. Stir in the remaining onions and season with salt and pepper. Refrigerate until cold, about 1 hour.

2. **MAKE THE FLATBREAD:** In a large bowl, whisk together the High-Protein Flour and salt. Add 295g of water, the yogurt, and olive oil; stir to combine. If the dough seems too dry, add the remaining 60g of water, 15g at a time, until the dough is soft and pliable; let sit for 3 minutes to thicken. Dust a clean work surface with High-Protein Flour and transfer the dough onto it. Using floured hands, knead the dough until smooth and elastic, about 1 minute.

3. **SHAPE:** Divide the dough into six equal pieces. Sprinkle the work surface with about 3g (1 teaspoon) of sesame seeds and, using a rolling pin, roll out one piece of dough on top of the sesame seeds into an oval about 10 inches long, 8 inches wide, and ⅓ inch thick.

4. **PREHEAT:** Set a dry cast-iron skillet over medium heat.

5. **COOK:** Place the dough oval into the hot pan and cook, turning once, until char marks appear on the bottom, about 3 minutes; transfer to a rimmed baking sheet. Repeat the rolling and cooking process with the remaining dough pieces and sesame seeds. Serve warm with the onion dip.

TIP: Prefer to bake these in your oven? Place an inverted rimmed baking sheet on the bottom rack of the oven and preheat to 475°F. A few minutes before baking, lightly spray the dough rounds with water and set them on a sheet of parchment paper (with the seeds either up or down). Transfer with the paper onto the preheated baking sheet and bake until lightly golden, about 3 minutes. Repeat with the remaining dough.

CLASSIC ENGLISH MUFFINS

I grew up on Thomas' English muffins. When I tried to make a gluten-free version, I had my hands full trying to get the quintessential nooks-and-crannies texture. My secret? Oats and millet—and if you can get your hands on it, brown rice farina, which replaces the glutenous semolina farina used in the original recipe. Swap in medium-grind cornmeal in a pinch.

YIELD: 12 (2½-inch) English muffins **ACTIVE TIME:** 15 minutes
COOK TIME: 1 hour **TOTAL TIME:** 2 hours 45 minutes

TOOLS NEEDED

kitchen scale

small bowl

stand mixer with paddle attachment or large bowl and dough whisk

rimmed baking sheet

parchment paper

nonstick cooking spray

twelve 3-inch English muffin rings or mason jar lid rings

plastic wrap

cast-iron skillet

spatula

wire rack

INGREDIENTS

22g hulled whole millet

550g Whole-Grain Flour (page 33)

24g gluten-free old-fashioned rolled oats

8g (2 teaspoons) granulated sugar

9g (1½ teaspoons) salt

2g (¾ teaspoon) cream of tartar

2g (½ teaspoon) baking soda

236g lukewarm water (65°F)

177g whole milk, heated to 100°F

12g canola oil

Brown rice farina, for scattering

1. **COMBINE:** In a small bowl, combine the millet and 59g (¼ cup) boiling water; let soak for 15 minutes, then drain. In a large bowl with a dough whisk or in the bowl of a stand mixer fitted with the paddle attachment, mix together the Whole-Grain Flour, oats, sugar, salt, cream of tartar, and baking soda. Add the lukewarm water, milk, canola oil, and soaked millet; mix until combined. Increase the speed to medium and beat for 3 minutes to add air to the dough.

2. **SHAPE:** Line a rimmed baking sheet with parchment paper and grease with nonstick cooking spray. Use the spray to coat the insides of 12 English muffin rings (or use the rings from 3-inch mason jar lids); place the rings on the prepared baking sheet and scatter with the farina to generously coat the surface of the baking sheet. Divide the dough into 12 equal pieces and place the dough inside the rings. Using greased hands, flatten the dough gently to fit the width of the ring. Grease the tops with cooking spray.

3. **PROOF:** Cover loosely with plastic wrap and let rise until puffy, about 1 hour.

4. **COOK:** Preheat the oven to 350°F, with a rack in the middle. Set a dry cast-iron skillet over medium-low heat for 3 minutes. Working in batches, place six of the dough rounds with their rings into the hot pan and cook, turning once, until golden, 5 to 8 minutes on each side. Using a spatula, transfer to the baking sheet and bake until the centers are cooked, about 6 minutes. Repeat with the remaining dough.

5. **COOL:** Let cool completely on a wire rack, about 30 minutes, or for 5 minutes and serve warm.

> **TIP:** You can cook these in the oven, too. Place an inverted rimmed baking sheet on the bottom rack of the oven and preheat to 400°F. Keep the dough with its rings on the parchment you used to proof and, a few minutes before baking, spritz each dough round with water. Cover the English muffins with a piece of parchment and set a baking sheet on top to keep them from rounding as they bake. Transfer everything onto the preheated baking sheet and bake for 10 minutes, then carefully remove the top baking sheet and bake until golden, about 8 minutes more.

APPLE FRITTER MONKEY-BREAD MUFFINS

I could never resist an apple fritter—a taste of autumn wrapped up in a doughy package of apples and cinnamon. As a baked goods lover, I've always preferred the corner pieces for their crispy, crunchy edges. That's why I bake the monkey bread in a muffin pan.

MAKES: 12 muffins **PREP TIME:** 25 minutes
BAKE TIME: 25 minutes **TOTAL TIME:** 2 hours 20 minutes

TOOLS NEEDED

kitchen scale

large resealable plastic bag

stand mixer with paddle attachment or large bowl and dough whisk

12-cup muffin pan

muffin liners

plastic wrap

rimmed baking sheet

wire rack (optional)

INGREDIENTS

For the apple mixture

1 large apple (such as Honey-crisp), peeled, cored, and cut into ¼-inch pieces

100g (½ cup) granulated sugar

100g (½ cup) packed brown sugar

8g (1 tablespoon) ground cinnamon

For the dough

550g High-Protein Flour (page 32), plus more for dusting

236g lukewarm water (65°F)

123g whole milk, heated to 100°F

2 large eggs (114g), at room temperature

60g unsalted butter, melted, plus more for dipping

1. **MAKE THE APPLE MIXTURE:** In a large resealable plastic bag, toss together the apples, granulated sugar, brown sugar, and cinnamon.

2. **COMBINE THE DOUGH:** In a large bowl with a dough whisk or in the bowl of a stand mixer fitted with the paddle attachment, mix together the High-Protein Flour, water, milk, eggs, and 60g of melted butter on low speed until combined. Increase the speed to medium and beat for 3 minutes to add air to the dough.

3. **SHAPE:** Line a 12-cup muffin pan with liners. Tear off about 1 tablespoon of dough, form it into a ball, dip it in melted butter, and toss it into the bag with the apple mixture to coat. Remove and place in the prepared muffin pan. Repeat with the remaining dough, filling each muffin cup with three dough balls and some apple pieces.

4. **PROOF:** Cover the muffin pan loosely with plastic wrap and proof at room temperature until puffy, about 1 hour.

5. **PREHEAT:** Place an inverted rimmed baking sheet on the middle rack of the oven and preheat to 425°F.

6. **BAKE:** Sprinkle each muffin generously with any remaining cinnamon-sugar and bake until golden, 20 to 25 minutes.

7. **COOL:** Eat warm or let cool completely, about 30 minutes, on a wire rack.

> **TIP:** Sweeten the deal by drizzling a little lemon icing over the top of the muffins. In a small bowl, combine 125g (1 cup) of confectioners' sugar with 43g (3 tablespoons) of freshly squeezed lemon juice, 15g (1 tablespoon) of water, and a pinch of salt. Whisk until smooth and drizzle the muffins while they're still warm.

PULL-APART BUTTERMILK BUNS

Two key ingredients make this recipe light and fluffy: instant potato flakes and buttermilk. The potato flakes add airiness and keep the rolls fresher longer. The acidity from the buttermilk gives the dough a lift as it proofs, delivering added fluffiness to the baked buns.

YIELD: 9 (3-ounce) buns **ACTIVE TIME:** 30 minutes
BAKE TIME: 25 minutes **TOTAL TIME:** 3 hours

TOOLS NEEDED

kitchen scale

stand mixer with paddle attachment or large bowl and dough whisk

8-by-8-inch baking dish

parchment paper

rolling pin

plastic wrap

rimmed baking sheet

pastry brush

wire rack (optional)

INGREDIENTS

300g All-Purpose Flour (page 31), plus more for dusting

16g nonfat milk powder

12g granulated sugar

11g instant potato flakes

7g (one ¼-ounce package) instant yeast

6g (1 teaspoon) salt, plus more for sprinkling

177g buttermilk, at room temperature (see Tip)

2 large egg whites (60g), at room temperature, lightly beaten, or 60g lukewarm water (65°F)

28g unsalted butter, at room temperature, plus more for greasing and brushing

1. **COMBINE:** In a large bowl with a dough whisk or in the bowl of a stand mixer fitted with the paddle attachment, mix together the All-Purpose Flour, milk powder, sugar, potato flakes, yeast, and salt on low speed until blended. With the machine running on medium speed, stream in the buttermilk, egg whites, and butter; mix until combined.

2. **SHAPE:** Grease an 8-inch square baking dish with butter. Cover a clean work surface with a large piece of parchment paper and lightly dust with All-Purpose Flour. Using a rolling pin, gently roll the dough into a square about 7½ inches wide and 3 inches thick. Cut the dough into nine equal squares about 2½ inches wide each and place them, evenly spaced, into the prepared baking dish.

3. **PROOF:** Cover loosely with plastic wrap and proof at room temperature until puffy, about 1½ hours.

4. **PREHEAT:** Place an inverted rimmed baking sheet on the middle rack of the oven and preheat to 350°F.

5. **BAKE:** Bake the rolls until golden and fluffy, about 25 minutes.

6. **COOL:** Remove from the oven, use a pastry brush to brush with butter, and sprinkle generously with salt. Eat warm or let cool completely, about 30 minutes, on a wire rack.

TIP: No buttermilk? Make your own. Stir together 184g (¾ cup) of milk and 12g (2½ teaspoons) apple cider vinegar. Let stand for 5 to 10 minutes to thicken before using.

TRIPLE BERRY CREAM CHEESE DANISHES

The berry-topped, slightly sweetened cream cheese cradled in brioche dough makes these danishes pure comfort. While the steps may seem daunting, I promise you the recipe is easier than it looks. You'll know the process is completely worth it after your first bite.

YIELD: 8 (2½-inch) danishes **ACTIVE TIME:** 30 minutes **BAKE TIME:** 25 minutes
TOTAL TIME: 7 hours 15 minutes to 11 hours 15 minutes
(depending on your proofing method)

TOOLS NEEDED

kitchen scale

stand mixer with paddle attachment or large bowl and dough whisk

plastic wrap

three small bowls

whisk

three rimmed baking sheets

parchment paper

nonstick cooking spray

two storage containers

spoon

pastry brush

small saucepan

wire rack

INGREDIENTS

For the dough

224g All-Purpose Flour (page 31), divided

50g whole milk, heated to 100°F

3g (1 teaspoon) instant yeast

3 large eggs (171g), at room temperature, divided

38g granulated sugar

3g (½ teaspoon) salt

85g unsalted butter, at room temperature

For the cream cheese filling

112g (½ cup) cream cheese, at room temperature

50g (¼ cup) granulated sugar

1 large egg yolk (18g), at room temperature

For the fruit filling

50g (¼ cup) granulated sugar

7g (1 tablespoon) cornstarch

Pinch salt

325g (about 2 cups) mixed berries, such as blackberries, blueberries, raspberries, and sliced strawberries (see Tip)

28g (2 tablespoons) freshly squeezed lemon juice

For the egg wash

1 large egg (57g), at room temperature

5g (1 teaspoon) water

Pinch salt

For the apricot glaze

20g (2 tablespoons) apricot jam

5g (1 teaspoon) water

1. **START THE DOUGH:** In a large bowl with a dough whisk or in the bowl of a stand mixer fitted with a paddle attachment, mix together 120g of All-Purpose Flour, the milk, yeast, and 1 egg (57g) on low speed. Increase the speed to medium and beat for 3 minutes to add air to the dough.

2. **PROOF:** Cover loosely with plastic wrap and proof at room temperature until the dough is puffy, about 40 minutes.

3. **FINISH THE DOUGH:** In a small bowl, lightly beat the remaining 2 eggs (114g). To the proofed dough, add 60g of All-Purpose Flour, the sugar, salt, and beaten eggs. Mix on low speed to combine, about 1 minute. With the motor running, gradually add the remaining 44g of All-Purpose Flour until combined, then increase the speed to medium and beat for 15 minutes

CONTINUED ▷

to add air to the dough, scraping down the bowl as needed. Reduce the speed to medium-low and gradually add the butter. Increase the speed to medium and beat for 5 minutes more to completely incorporate, scraping down the bowl as needed.

4. **SHAPE:** Line a rimmed baking sheet with parchment paper. Divide the dough into eight equal pieces and place them about 2 inches apart on the prepared baking sheet.

5. **PROOF:** Cover loosely with plastic wrap and proof at room temperature until the dough is puffy, about 1½ hours. Grease the dough with non-stick cooking spray and cover tightly with plastic wrap; refrigerate for 4 to 6 hours or, for a lighter texture, overnight.

6. **MAKE THE CREAM CHEESE FILLING:** In a large bowl with a dough whisk or in the bowl of a stand mixer fitted with a paddle attachment, mix together the cream cheese and sugar on low speed until combined. Add the egg yolk and mix, scraping down the sides of the bowl if necessary, until just combined. Transfer to a storage container and refrigerate until set, about 2 hours.

7. **MAKE THE FRUIT FILLING:** Preheat the oven to 375°F. Line a second rimmed baking sheet with parchment paper. In a second small bowl, whisk together the sugar, cornstarch, and salt. Place the berries on the prepared baking sheet, sprinkle them with the sugar mixture, toss to coat, then drizzle with lemon juice. Bake until softened, about 20 minutes. Let cool slightly, then transfer to a second storage container and refrigerate until cooled completely, about 1 hour.

8. **PREHEAT:** Remove the dough from the refrigerator and return to room temperature, about 1 hour. Meanwhile, place an inverted third rimmed baking sheet on the middle rack of the oven and preheat to 350°F.

9. **MAKE THE EGG WASH:** In a third small bowl, whisk together the egg, water, and salt.

10. **BAKE:** Using a wet spoon, gently press down the surface of each dough portion to make an indentation, leaving about a 1-inch border of dough. Fill with about 1 tablespoon of the cream cheese filling and 2 tablespoons of the berry filling. Using a pastry brush, gently coat the dough with the egg wash. Transfer the baking sheet onto the preheated baking sheet and bake until golden, about 25 minutes.

11. **MAKE THE APRICOT GLAZE:** Combine the jam and water in a small saucepan and heat over medium-low heat, stirring, until warmed, about 3 minutes.

12. **COOL:** Place the baking sheet on a wire rack and, using a pastry brush, coat the danishes with the apricot glaze. Serve warm or let cool completely, about 45 minutes.

TIP: Switch it up by swapping in your favorite seasonal fruit, like apples, or removing the fruit altogether for a classic cream cheese danish.

SOURDOUGH CHOCOLATE FOUGASSE, PAGE 122

CHAPTER 6

PRE-FERMENTED AND SOURDOUGH BREADS

To make the recipes in this chapter, I use an easy overnight starter called a poolish. But instead of making a new starter each time, you can also create and maintain a sourdough starter following the step-by-step directions on page 19. If you do, skip step 1 in each of the recipes in this chapter.

CLASSIC SOURDOUGH LOAF

For this low-maintenance sourdough loaf, I use a proofing basket called a brotform, lined with a floured kitchen towel, to make transferring the dough easy.

YIELD: 1 (2-pound) loaf **ACTIVE TIME:** 15 minutes **BAKE TIME:** 1 hour 20 minutes
TOTAL TIME: 14 to 26 hours (depending on your starter)

TOOLS NEEDED

kitchen scale

medium bowl and plastic wrap or sealable container

stand mixer with paddle attachment or large bowl and dough whisk

7-inch proofing basket (optional)

kitchen towel

offset spatula or spoon

plastic wrap

rimmed baking sheet

parchment paper

bread lame or sharp knife

14.3-by-3.6-by-10.6-inch nonstick parchment paper cooking bag

heatproof clip (optional)

wire rack

INGREDIENTS

For the starter

125g High-Protein Flour (page 32)

1g (¼ teaspoon) instant yeast

125g lukewarm water (65°F)

For the dough

415g High-Protein Flour (page 32), plus more for dusting

3g (½ teaspoon) salt

1g (¼ teaspoon) instant yeast

350g lukewarm water (65°F)

1. **COMBINE THE STARTER:** In a medium bowl or sealable container, stir together the High-Protein Flour and yeast. Stir in the water until combined. Seal or cover tightly with plastic wrap and let sit at room temperature until bubbles appear on the surface, about 12 hours.

2. **COMBINE THE DOUGH:** In a large bowl using a dough whisk or in the bowl of a stand mixer fitted with the paddle attachment, mix together the High-Protein Flour, salt, and yeast on low speed. Add the water and mix until combined. Increase the speed to medium and beat for 3 minutes to add air to the dough. Reduce the speed to low and gradually add the starter; mix until just combined.

3. **SHAPE:** Line a 7-inch proofing basket with a clean kitchen towel and dust generously with High-Protein Flour. (If you don't have a proofing basket, cradle the dough in a generously floured kitchen towel instead). Transfer the dough into the basket and, using a wet offset spatula or spoon, gently smooth out the surface and dust with High-Protein Flour.

4. **PROOF:** Cover the dough loosely with plastic wrap and proof at room temperature until the dough is puffy, about 1½ hours, then transfer to the refrigerator and proof for at least 10 hours (or up to 18 hours for a richer sourdough flavor).

5. **PREHEAT:** Remove the dough from the refrigerator and return to room temperature, about 1 hour. Place an inverted rimmed baking sheet on the lower third rack of the oven and preheat to 450°F. When the oven is preheated, gently invert the dough onto a piece of parchment paper and lightly dust the top with High-Protein Flour. Using a sharp knife or bread lame, score the surface with a crosshatch or leaf design and slide the dough with its parchment paper into a parchment paper cooking bag; fold the bag opening several turns or use a heatproof clip to seal.

6. **BAKE:** Reduce the heat to 425°F and place the cooking bag on the pre-heated baking sheet. Bake until the loaf is crusty and sounds hollow when tapped on the bottom, about 1 hour 20 minutes.

7. **COOL:** Carefully tear open the bag (hot steam will escape), remove the loaf, and let cool completely, about 1 hour, on a wire rack before slicing.

SOURDOUGH FRENCH BAGUETTE

I love the versatility of a baguette. Think garlic bread, crostini, and of course, cheesy toppers for French onion soup. If you want to make multiple baguettes, just double the recipe and preheat a second inverted rimmed baking sheet. Place the baking sheets on two separate oven racks positioned in the top and bottom thirds of your oven.

YIELD: 1 (14-inch) baguette **ACTIVE TIME:** 10 minutes **BAKE TIME:** 40 minutes
TOTAL TIME: 15 to 24 hours (depending on your proofing method)

TOOLS NEEDED

kitchen scale

medium bowl and plastic wrap or sealable container

stand mixer with paddle attachment or large bowl and dough whisk

parchment paper

offset spatula or spoon

plastic wrap

rimmed baking sheet

bread lame or sharp knife

14.3-by-3.6-by-10.6-inch nonstick parchment paper cooking bag

heatproof clip (optional)

wire rack

INGREDIENTS

For the starter

60g High-Protein Flour (page 32)

1g (¼ teaspoon) instant yeast

60g lukewarm water (65°F)

For the dough

220g High-Protein Flour (page 32), plus more for dusting

3g (½ teaspoon) salt

160g lukewarm water (65°F)

2 large egg whites (60g), at room temperature, or 60g more lukewarm water (65°F)

14g olive oil

2g (½ teaspoon) apple cider vinegar

1. **COMBINE THE STARTER:** In a medium bowl or sealable container, stir together the High-Protein Flour and yeast. Stir in the water until combined. Seal or cover tightly with plastic wrap and let sit at room temperature until bubbles appear on the surface, about 12 hours.

2. **COMBINE THE DOUGH:** In a large bowl using a dough whisk or in the bowl of a stand mixer fitted with the paddle attachment, mix together the High-Protein Flour and salt on low speed. Add the water, egg whites, starter, olive oil, and vinegar; mix until combined. Increase the speed to medium and beat for 3 minutes to add air to the dough.

3. **SHAPE:** Generously dust a piece of parchment paper with High-Protein Flour. Transfer the dough to the parchment paper and, using your hands, stretch and roll the dough into a baguette shape about 14 inches long. Using a wet offset spatula or spoon, gently smooth out the surface of the dough.

4. **PROOF:** Cover loosely with plastic wrap and proof at room temperature until the dough is puffy, about 1½ hours. (If desired, refrigerate for 8 hours or overnight. Return to room temperature, about 1 hour, before baking.)

5. **PREHEAT:** Place an inverted rimmed baking sheet on the middle rack of the oven and preheat to 450°F. Using a sharp knife or bread lame, score the surface crosswise with three diagonal slashes. Spritz the dough with water and slide the dough with its parchment paper into a parchment paper cooking bag; fold the bag opening several turns or use a heatproof clip to seal.

6. **BAKE:** Reduce the heat to 425°F and place the cooking bag on the preheated baking sheet. Bake until the baguette is crusty and sounds hollow when tapped on the bottom, about 40 minutes.

7. **COOL:** Carefully tear open the bag (hot steam will escape), remove the loaf, and let cool completely, about 40 minutes, on a wire rack before slicing.

CRANBERRY-PECAN SOURDOUGH ROLLS

These rolls are a Thanksgiving favorite. For a deeper sourdough flavor, refrigerate for 8 hours and up to overnight in step 4.

YIELD: 4 (4-ounce) rolls **ACTIVE TIME:** 10 minutes **BAKE TIME:** 30 minutes
TOTAL TIME: 14 hours 20 minutes to 23 hours 20 minutes
(depending on your proofing method)

TOOLS NEEDED

kitchen scale

medium bowl with plastic wrap or sealable container

stand mixer with paddle attachment or large bowl and dough whisk

parchment paper

3-ounce ice cream scoop or ⅓ cup measuring cup

offset spatula or spoon

rimmed baking sheet

14.3-by-3.6-by-10.6-inch nonstick parchment paper cooking bag

heatproof clip (optional)

wire rack

INGREDIENTS

For the starter

60g Whole-Grain Flour (page 33)

1g (¼ teaspoon) instant yeast

60g lukewarm water (65°F)

For the dough

220g Whole-Grain Flour (page 33), plus more for dusting

3g (½ teaspoon) salt

140g lukewarm water (65°F)

21g honey

2 large egg whites (60g), at room temperature, or 60g more lukewarm water (65°F)

14g sunflower seed oil

2g (½ teaspoon) apple cider vinegar

70g dried cranberries

65g chopped pecans (see Tip)

1. **COMBINE THE STARTER:** In a medium bowl or sealable container, stir together the Whole-Grain Flour and yeast. Stir in the water until combined. Seal or cover tightly with plastic wrap and let sit at room temperature until bubbles appear on the surface, about 12 hours.

2. **COMBINE THE DOUGH:** In a large bowl using a dough whisk or in the bowl of a stand mixer fitted with the paddle attachment, mix together the Whole-Grain Flour and salt on low speed. Add the water, honey, egg whites, starter, sunflower seed oil, and vinegar; mix until combined. Increase the speed to medium and beat for 3 minutes to add air to the dough. Reduce the speed to low and mix in the cranberries and pecans until just combined.

3. **SHAPE:** Generously dust a piece of parchment paper with Whole-Grain Flour. Using a wet 3-ounce ice cream scoop or ⅓ measuring cup, scoop the dough onto the parchment paper, spacing the rolls about 2 inches apart. Using a wet offset spatula or spoon, gently smooth out the surface of each roll.

4. **PROOF:** Cover loosely with plastic wrap and proof at room temperature until the dough is puffy, about 1½ hours. (If desired, refrigerate for 8 hours or overnight. Return to room temperature, about 1 hour, before baking.)

5. **PREHEAT:** Place an inverted rimmed baking sheet on the middle rack of the oven and preheat to 400°F. Lightly dust the top of the rolls with Whole-Grain Flour and slide the dough with its parchment into a parchment paper cooking bag; fold the bag opening several turns or use a heatproof clip to seal.

6. **BAKE:** Place the cooking bag on the preheated baking sheet and bake until golden, about 30 minutes.

7. **COOL:** Carefully tear open the bag (hot steam will escape), remove the loaf, and let cool slightly, about 10 minutes, on a wire rack.

TIP: Not a pecan lover? Swap in walnuts.

SOURDOUGH BIALY BREAD SLABS

Making bialys is similar to bagels except that there's no need to boil the dough before baking. The key to the bialy's signature shape is in how you place the onion filling. I like to gently press down the center of each dough round until it's thin enough that it won't rise too much for the filling to stay in place.

YIELD: 6 (4-ounce) bialys **ACTIVE TIME:** 20 minutes
BAKE TIME: 25 minutes **TOTAL TIME:** 14 hours 15 minutes

TOOLS NEEDED

kitchen scale

medium bowl and plastic wrap or sealable container

medium skillet

stand mixer with paddle attachment or large bowl and dough whisk

rimmed baking sheet

parchment paper

nonstick cooking spray

plastic wrap

small bowl

whisk

pastry brush

wire rack

INGREDIENTS

For the starter

60g Whole-Grain Flour (page 33)

1g (¼ teaspoon) instant yeast

60g lukewarm water (65°F)

For the filling

24g (2 tablespoons) olive oil

1 medium white onion, chopped (about 100g)

18g (2 tablespoons) poppy seeds, plus more for sprinkling

Salt

For the dough

220g Whole-Grain Flour (page 33), plus more for dusting

3g (½ teaspoon) salt

140g lukewarm water (65°F)

21g honey

3 large egg whites (90g), at room temperature, or 90g more lukewarm water (65°F), divided

14g sunflower seed oil

2g (½ teaspoon) apple cider vinegar

1. **COMBINE THE STARTER:** In a medium bowl or sealable container, stir together the Whole-Grain Flour and yeast. Stir in the water until combined. Seal or cover tightly with plastic wrap and let sit at room temperature until bubbles appear on the surface, about 12 hours.

2. **MAKE THE FILLING:** In a medium skillet over medium-low heat, heat the olive oil. Add the onion and cook, stirring occasionally, until golden, about 12 minutes. Stir in the poppy seeds and a pinch of salt. Remove from the heat and set aside.

3. **COMBINE THE DOUGH:** In a large bowl with a dough whisk or in the bowl of a stand mixer fitted with the paddle attachment, mix together the Whole-Grain Flour and salt on low speed. Add the water, honey, 2 egg whites (60g), starter, sunflower seed oil, and vinegar; mix until combined. Increase the speed to medium and beat for 3 minutes to add air to the dough.

4. **SHAPE:** Line a rimmed baking sheet with parchment paper and grease with nonstick cooking spray. Divide the dough into six equal pieces and shape each into a ball. Place the shaped dough about 2 inches apart on the prepared baking sheet and grease with cooking spray. Using your finger, make in indentation in the center of each dough ball, leaving a 1-inch border of dough around the edges and making sure not to poke through the dough; evenly divide the filling among the dough pieces.

5. **PROOF:** Cover loosely with plastic wrap and proof at room temperature until the dough is puffy, about 1½ hours.

6. **PREHEAT:** Preheat the oven to 475°F.

CONTINUED ▷

7. **MAKE THE EGG WASH:** In a small bowl, beat the remaining egg white (30g) lightly with 15g (1 tablespoon) water. Use a pastry brush to coat the bialys with the egg wash and sprinkle with poppy seeds.

8. **BAKE:** Reduce the heat to 425°F and bake until browned, about 25 minutes.

9. **COOL:** Let cool on a wire rack for 10 minutes and serve warm or at room temperature.

TIP: Take this bialy bread over the top—stir in about 24g cooked bacon bits to the filling.

ASIAGO SOURDOUGH CIABATTA

This recipe was inspired by the sudden popularity of Asiago cheese bread in cafes across America. The first time I tasted it was at Panera Bread before Isaiah was diagnosed with gluten intolerance. I've been making iterations of it ever since.

YIELD: 1 (1-pound) loaf **ACTIVE TIME:** 15 minutes **BAKE TIME:** 1 hour 20 minutes
TOTAL TIME: 15 hours 35 minutes to 24 hours 35 minutes
(depending on your proofing method)

TOOLS NEEDED

kitchen scale

medium bowl and plastic wrap or sealable container

stand mixer with paddle attachment or large bowl and dough whisk

parchment paper

offset spatula or spoon

plastic wrap

rimmed baking sheet

cheese grater

14.3-by-3.6-by-10.6-inch nonstick parchment paper cooking bag

heatproof clip (optional)

wire rack

INGREDIENTS

For the starter

60g High-Protein Flour (page 32)

1g (¼ teaspoon) instant yeast

60g lukewarm water (65°F)

CONTINUED ▷

For the dough

220g High-Protein Flour (page 32), plus more for dusting

3g (½ teaspoon) salt

140g lukewarm water (65°F)

2 large egg whites (60g), at room temperature, or 60g more lukewarm water (65°F)

14g olive oil

2g (½ teaspoon) apple cider vinegar

56g Asiago cheese, cut into ¼-inch cubes, plus more for grating (see Tip)

1. **COMBINE THE STARTER:** In a medium bowl or sealable container, stir together the High-Protein Flour and yeast. Stir in the water until combined. Seal or cover tightly with plastic wrap and let sit at room temperature until bubbles appear on the surface, about 12 hours.

2. **COMBINE THE DOUGH:** In a large bowl using a dough whisk or in the bowl of a stand mixer fitted with the paddle attachment, mix together the High-Protein Flour and salt on low speed. Add the water, egg whites, starter, olive oil and vinegar; mix until combined. Increase the speed to medium and beat for 3 minutes to add air to the dough. Reduce the speed to low and mix in the cheese until just combined.

3. **SHAPE:** Generously dust a piece of parchment paper with High-Protein Flour; place the dough onto the parchment paper. Using a wet offset spatula or a spoon, shape the dough into a loaf and gently smooth out the surface.

4. **PROOF:** Cover loosely with plastic wrap and proof at room temperature until the dough is puffy, about 1½ hours. (If desired, refrigerate for 8 hours or overnight. Return to room temperature, about 1 hour, before baking.)

5. **PREHEAT:** Place an inverted rimmed baking sheet on the middle rack of the oven and preheat to 400°F. Spray the dough with water and, using a cheese grater, top with shredded cheese to taste and dust with High-Protein Flour. Slide the dough with its parchment into a parchment paper cooking bag; fold the bag opening several turns or use a heatproof clip to seal.

6. **BAKE:** Place the cooking bag on the preheated baking sheet and bake until the loaf is crusty and sounds hollow when tapped on the bottom, about 1 hour 20 minutes.

7. **COOL:** Carefully tear open the bag (hot steam will escape), remove the loaf, and let cool completely, about 30 minutes, on a wire rack before slicing.

TIP: Swap in another Italian cheese, like Parmesan or Pecorino, for the Asiago if you prefer.

BUFFALO-GORGONZOLA SOURDOUGH LOAF

This loaf is perfect to serve alongside a platter of chicken wings for your next Super Bowl Sunday or to dunk into a comforting bowl of tomato bisque.

YIELD: 1 (1-pound) loaf **ACTIVE TIME:** 15 minutes **BAKE TIME:** 1 hour 20 minutes
TOTAL TIME: 15 hours 35 minutes to 24 hours 35 minutes
(depending on your proofing method)

TOOLS NEEDED

kitchen scale

medium bowl and plastic wrap or sealable container

stand mixer with paddle attachment or large bowl and dough whisk

parchment paper

offset spatula or spoon

rimmed baking sheet

14.3-by-3.6-by-10.6-inch nonstick parchment paper cooking bag

heatproof clip (optional)

wire rack

INGREDIENTS

For the starter

60g Whole-Grain Flour (page 33)

1g (¼ teaspoon) instant yeast

60g lukewarm water (65°F)

For the dough

220g Whole-Grain Flour (page 33), plus more for dusting

6g (2 teaspoons) buffalo wing seasoning

3g (½ teaspoon) salt

140g lukewarm water (65°F)

2 large egg whites (60g), at room temperature, or 60g more lukewarm water (65°F)

14g sunflower seed oil

2g (½ teaspoon) apple cider vinegar

56g Gorgonzola cheese crumbles

1. **COMBINE THE STARTER:** In a medium bowl or sealable container, stir together the Whole-Grain Flour and yeast. Stir in the water until combined. Seal or cover tightly with plastic wrap and let sit at room temperature until bubbles appear on the surface, about 12 hours.

2. **COMBINE THE DOUGH:** In a large bowl using a dough whisk or in the bowl of a stand mixer fitted with the paddle attachment, mix together the Whole-Grain Flour, buffalo wing seasoning, and salt on low speed. Add the water, egg whites, starter, sunflower seed oil, and vinegar; mix until combined. Increase the speed to medium and beat for 3 minutes to add air to the dough. Reduce the speed to low and mix in the cheese until just combined.

3. **SHAPE:** Generously dust a piece of parchment paper with Whole-Grain Flour; place the dough onto the parchment paper. Using a wet offset spatula or a spoon, shape the dough into a loaf and gently smooth out the surface.

4. **PROOF:** Cover loosely with plastic wrap and proof at room temperature until the dough is puffy, about 1½ hours. (If desired, refrigerate for 8 hours or overnight. Return to room temperature, about 1 hour, before baking.)

5. **PREHEAT:** Place an inverted rimmed baking sheet on the middle rack of the oven and preheat to 400°F. Slide the dough with its parchment into a parchment paper cooking bag; fold the bag opening several turns or use a heatproof clip to seal.

6. **BAKE:** Place the cooking bag on the preheated baking sheet and bake until the loaf is crusty and sounds hollow when tapped on the bottom, about 1 hour 20 minutes.

7. **COOL:** Carefully tear open the bag (hot steam will escape), remove the loaf, and let cool completely, about 30 minutes, on a wire rack before slicing.

TIP: Prefer a milder cheese? Swap in feta or goat cheese crumbles instead.

SUN-DRIED TOMATO AND PARMESAN SOURDOUGH BREAD

This cheesy bread is studded with pieces of sun-dried tomato, which give the bread a wonderfully sweet-tart flavor. If you're dairy-free, swap in roasted garlic for the Parmesan.

YIELD: 1 (1-pound) loaf **ACTIVE TIME:** 15 minutes **BAKE TIME:** 1 hour 20 minutes
TOTAL TIME: 15 hours 35 minutes to 24 hours 35 minutes
(depending on your proofing method)

TOOLS NEEDED

kitchen scale

medium bowl and plastic wrap or sealable container

stand mixer with paddle attachment or large bowl and dough whisk

parchment paper

offset spatula or spoon

plastic wrap

rimmed baking sheet

14.3-by-3.6-by-10.6-inch nonstick parchment paper cooking bag

heatproof clip (optional)

wire rack

INGREDIENTS

For the starter

60g Whole-Grain Flour (page 33)

1g (¼ teaspoon) instant yeast

60g lukewarm water (65°F)

For the dough

220g Whole-Grain Flour (page 33), plus more for dusting

3g (½ teaspoon) salt

3g (½ teaspoon) Italian seasoning, plus more for sprinkling

140g lukewarm water (65°F)

2 large egg whites (60g), at room temperature, or 60g more lukewarm water (65°F)

14g olive oil, plus more for brushing

2g (½ teaspoon) apple cider vinegar

28g sun-dried tomatoes, finely chopped

22g grated Parmesan cheese, plus more for sprinkling (see Tip)

1. **COMBINE THE STARTER:** In a medium bowl or sealable container, stir together the Whole-Grain Flour and yeast. Stir in the water until combined. Seal or cover tightly with plastic wrap and let sit at room temperature until bubbles appear on the surface, about 12 hours.

2. **COMBINE THE DOUGH:** In a large bowl using a dough whisk or in the bowl of a stand mixer fitted with the paddle attachment, mix together the Whole-Grain Flour, salt, and Italian seasoning on low speed. Add the water, egg whites, starter, oil, and vinegar; mix until combined. Increase the speed to medium and beat for 3 minutes to add air to the dough. Reduce the speed to low and mix in the tomatoes and cheese until just combined.

3. **SHAPE:** Generously dust a piece of parchment paper with Whole-Grain Flour; place the dough onto the parchment. Using a wet offset spatula or a spoon, shape the dough into a loaf and gently smooth out the surface.

4. **PROOF:** Cover loosely with plastic wrap and proof at room temperature until the dough is puffy, about 1½ hours. (If desired, refrigerate for 8 hours or overnight. Return to room temperature, about 1 hour, before baking.)

5. **PREHEAT:** Place an inverted rimmed baking sheet on the middle rack of the oven and preheat to 400°F. Brush the dough with olive oil and sprinkle with Parmesan and Italian seasoning. Slide the dough with its parchment into a parchment paper cooking bag; fold the bag opening several turns or use a heatproof clip to seal.

6. **BAKE:** Place the cooking bag on the preheated baking sheet and bake until the loaf is crusty and sounds hollow when tapped on the bottom, about 1 hour 20 minutes.

7. **COOL:** Carefully tear open the bag (hot steam will escape), remove the loaf, and let cool completely, about 30 minutes, on a wire rack before slicing.

CORNMEAL-ROSEMARY SOURDOUGH BREAD

This is my go-to summer bread, which I like to grill and top with sliced tomatoes, basil, a drizzle of olive oil, and a sprinkle of salt.

YIELD: 1 (1-pound) loaf **ACTIVE TIME:** 15 minutes
BAKE TIME: 1 hour 20 minutes **TOTAL TIME:** 15 hours 35 minutes to 24 hours 35 minutes (depending on your proofing method)

TOOLS NEEDED

kitchen scale

medium bowl and plastic wrap or sealable container

stand mixer with paddle attachment or large bowl and dough whisk

parchment paper

offset spatula or spoon

plastic wrap

rimmed baking sheet

bread lame or sharp knife

14.3-by-3.6-by-10.6-inch nonstick parchment paper cooking bag

heatproof clip (optional)

wire rack

INGREDIENTS

For the starter

60g High-Protein Flour (page 32)

1g (¼ teaspoon) instant yeast

60g lukewarm water (65°F)

For the dough

220g High-Protein Flour (page 32)

50g medium-grind cornmeal, plus more for dusting

3g (½ teaspoon) salt

140g lukewarm water (65°F)

2 large egg whites (60g), at room temperature, or 60g more lukewarm water (65°F)

12g sunflower seed oil

2g (½ teaspoon) apple cider vinegar

2g (1 tablespoon) chopped fresh rosemary

1. **COMBINE THE STARTER:** In a medium bowl or sealable container, stir together the High-Protein Flour and yeast. Stir in the water until combined. Seal or cover tightly with plastic wrap and let sit at room temperature until bubbles appear on the surface, about 12 hours.

2. **COMBINE THE DOUGH:** In a large bowl using a dough whisk or in the bowl of a stand mixer fitted with the paddle attachment, mix together the High-Protein Flour, cornmeal, and salt on low speed. Add the water, egg whites, starter, sunflower seed oil, vinegar, and rosemary; mix until combined. Increase the speed to medium and beat for 3 minutes to add air to the dough.

3. **SHAPE:** Generously dust a piece of parchment paper with cornmeal; place the dough onto the parchment paper. Using a wet offset spatula or a spoon, shape the dough into a loaf and gently smooth out the surface.

4. **PROOF:** Cover loosely with plastic wrap and proof at room temperature until the dough is puffy, about 1½ hours. (If desired, refrigerate for 8 hours or overnight. Return to room temperature, about 1 hour, before baking.)

5. **PREHEAT:** Place an inverted rimmed baking sheet on the middle rack of the oven and preheat to 400°F. Spray the dough with water, then dust generously with cornmeal and, using a sharp knife or bread lame, make a ¼-inch-deep slash lengthwise along its center. Slide the dough with its parchment into a parchment paper cooking bag; fold the bag opening several turns or use a heatproof clip to seal.

6. **BAKE:** Place the cooking bag on the preheated baking sheet and bake until the loaf is crusty and sounds hollow when tapped on the bottom, about 1 hour 20 minutes.

7. **COOL:** Carefully tear open the bag (hot steam will escape), remove the loaf, and let cool completely, about 30 minutes, on a wire rack before slicing.

> **TIP:** Add 2g (1 teaspoon) grated orange zest to the dough for another layer of flavor.

SOURDOUGH CHOCOLATE FOUGASSE

I can't imagine a cookbook without chocolate, and there's no better bread for it than fougasse, which is a leaf-shaped bread similar in texture to focaccia or even breadsticks.

YIELD: 1 (1-pound) loaf **ACTIVE TIME:** 20 minutes **BAKE TIME:** 30 minutes
TOTAL TIME: 14 hours 30 minutes to 23 hours 30 minutes
(depending on your proofing method)

TOOLS NEEDED

kitchen scale

medium bowl and plastic wrap or sealable container

stand mixer with paddle attachment or large bowl and dough whisk

parchment paper

rolling pin (optional)

offset spatula or spoon

sharp knife

two rimmed baking sheets

plastic wrap

wire rack

INGREDIENTS

For the starter

60g Whole-Grain Flour (page 33)

1g (¼ teaspoon) instant yeast

60g lukewarm water (65°F)

For the dough

220g Whole-Grain Flour (page 33), plus more for dusting

3g (½ teaspoon) salt

140g lukewarm water (65°F)

2 large egg whites (60g), at room temperature, or 60g more lukewarm water (65°F)

21g honey

14g unsalted butter, melted

2g (½ teaspoon) apple cider vinegar

34g chopped semi sweet chocolate chips

Confectioners' sugar, for dusting

1. **COMBINE THE STARTER:** In a medium bowl or sealable container, stir together the Whole-Grain Flour and yeast. Stir in the water until combined. Seal or cover tightly with plastic wrap and let sit at room temperature until bubbles appear on the surface, about 12 hours.

2. **COMBINE THE DOUGH:** In a large bowl using a dough whisk or in the bowl of a stand mixer fitted with the paddle attachment, mix together the Whole-Grain Flour and salt on low speed. Add the water, egg whites, honey, starter, butter, and vinegar; mix until combined. Increase the speed to medium and beat for 3 minutes to add air to the dough. Reduce the speed to low and mix in the chocolate until just combined.

3. **SHAPE:** Dust a piece of parchment paper with Whole-Grain Flour; place the dough onto the parchment and dust with more Whole-Grain Flour. Using your fingertips or a flour-dusted rolling pin, shape the dough into an oval. Using a wet offset spatula or a spoon, gently smooth out the surface. Using a sharp knife, cut a slit lengthwise through the center and three diagonal slits, about an inch apart, on either side, leaving 1 inch of dough on either end of each slit). Using floured hands, gently stretch the dough until there is a 2-inch space between each slit. Carefully transfer the dough with its parchment onto a rimmed baking sheet.

4. **PROOF:** Cover loosely with plastic wrap and proof at room temperature until the dough is puffy, about 1½ hours. (If desired, refrigerate for 8 hours or overnight. Return to room temperature, about 1 hour, before baking.)

5. **PREHEAT:** Place an inverted rimmed baking sheet on the middle rack of the oven and preheat to 400°F.

6. **BAKE:** Place the baking sheet with dough onto the preheated baking sheet and bake until golden, about 30 minutes.

7. **COOL:** Let cool for 10 minutes on a wire rack. Dust with confectioners' sugar.

GUIDE TO HIGH-ALTITUDE BAKING

With high altitude comes low air pressure, meaning baked goods may not react the same way they do at sea level. If you first try the recipe as written and find it needs adjustment, here is a guide to help you.

To learn more about high-altitude baking, look to the Colorado State University Extension's *High Altitude Food Preparation* guide, available for no charge online.

BAKING SODA: This will need to be reduced in recipes based on your elevation. If the recipe calls for 1 teaspoon, reduce that to ⅞ teaspoon at 3,000 to 5,000 feet, ½ teaspoon at 5,000 to 6,000 feet, and ¼ teaspoon at 6,500 to 8,000 feet.

BAKING TIME: This should be decreased by 5 to 7 minutes for each 30 minutes of baking time. For example, if a recipe calls for 30 minutes in the oven, decrease the baking time to 23 to 25 minutes. The lower air pressure at higher elevation makes baking happen quicker.

FLOUR: An additional 1 tablespoon of flour may be helpful in recipes baked above 3,500 feet. For each additional 1,500 feet in elevation, add 1 tablespoon of flour.

LIQUID: Increase the liquid in a recipe by 1 to 2 tablespoons (15 to 30 ml) at 3,000-feet elevation. Above 3,000 feet, increase the liquid by 1½ teaspoons for each additional 1,000 feet of elevation to address evaporation.

OVEN TEMPERATURE: This can be increased by 15°F for most baked goods and by 25°F when making breads that contain chocolate. A higher temperature provides a quick set to your baked goods, reducing the amount of moisture lost during baking.

SUGAR: Reduce the amount of sugar in a recipe by 1 tablespoon per cup (or about 6 percent). The reason for this is much like oven temperature—more sugar increases the evaporation in baked goods. Lowering the amount of sugar may strengthen the structure and keep it moist.

MEASUREMENT CONVERSIONS

VOLUME EQUIVALENTS	U.S. STANDARD	U.S. STANDARD (OUNCES)	METRIC (APPROXIMATE)
LIQUID	2 tablespoons	1 fl. oz.	30 mL
	¼ cup	2 fl. oz.	60 mL
	½ cup	4 fl. oz.	120 mL
	1 cup	8 fl. oz.	240 mL
	1½ cups	12 fl. oz.	355 mL
	2 cups or 1 pint	16 fl. oz.	475 mL
	4 cups or 1 quart	32 fl. oz.	1 L
	1 gallon	128 fl. oz.	4 L
DRY	⅛ teaspoon	—	0.5 mL
	¼ teaspoon	—	1 mL
	½ teaspoon	—	2 mL
	¾ teaspoon	—	4 mL
	1 teaspoon	—	5 mL
	1 tablespoon	—	15 mL
	¼ cup	—	59 mL
	⅓ cup	—	79 mL
	½ cup	—	118 mL
	⅔ cup	—	156 mL
	¾ cup	—	177 mL
	1 cup	—	235 mL
	2 cups or 1 pint	—	475 mL
	3 cups	—	700 mL
	4 cups or 1 quart	—	1 L
	½ gallon	—	2 L
	1 gallon	—	4 L

OVEN TEMPERATURES

FAHRENHEIT	CELSIUS (APPROXIMATE)
250°F	120°C
300°F	150°C
325°F	165°C
350°F	180°C
375°F	190°C
400°F	200°C
425°F	220°C
450°F	230°C

WEIGHT EQUIVALENTS

U.S. STANDARD	METRIC (APPROXIMATE)
½ ounce	15 g
1 ounce	30 g
2 ounces	60 g
4 ounces	115 g
8 ounces	225 g
12 ounces	340 g
16 ounces or 1 pound	455 g

RESOURCES

AMAZON (Amazon.com)
Amazon is your best bet to find all the gluten-free ingredients and baking tools you need. You can also shop at your local health food and cookware stores.

BEYOND CELIAC (BeyondCeliac.org)
For more than 15 years, this organization has been helping people with celiac disease. Visit their site for info on what it means to live gluten-free, from food shopping and cross-contamination to entertaining and baking.

CULTURES FOR HEALTH (CulturesForHealth.com/learn/gf-sourdough/guide -binders-gluten-free-sourdough-baking)
This sustainable living company that sells gut-loving foods explains and defines gluten-free binders.

SCHÄR (Schaer.com/en-us/a/gluten-free-flours)
In "An In-Depth Guide to 12 Popular Gluten Free Flours," this international gluten-free food company outlines various naturally gluten-free flour options.

NATIONAL LIBRARY OF MEDICINE (PubMed.ncbi.nlm.nih.gov/19782179)
The "Psyllium as a Substitute for Gluten in Bread" study evaluates the effect of replacing gluten with psyllium in bread dough and the resulting loaf characteristics.

INDEX

About the Author

SILVANA NARDONE is the author of several cookbooks, including *Dairy-Free Meal Prep: Easy, Budget-Friendly Meals to Cook, Prep, Grab, and Go*; *The 30-Minute Dairy-Free Cookbook: 101 Easy and Delicious Meals for Busy People*; *Silvana's Gluten-Free and Dairy-Free Kitchen: Timeless Favorites Transformed*; and *Cooking for Isaiah: Gluten-Free & Dairy-Free Recipes for Easy, Delicious Meals*. She successfully launched Cooking for Isaiah®, a gluten-free, dairy-free flour blend and baking mix company that gives people the freedom to cook and bake again. Previously, Silvana was the founding editor-in-chief of celebrity chef Rachael Ray's magazine, *Rachael Ray Every Day*, and the owner of an Italian bakery, Fanciulla. She lives in New York City.